The Man Who Swam *into* History

Jewish History, Life, and Culture
MICHAEL NEIDITCH, Series Editor

The Man Who Swam *into* History

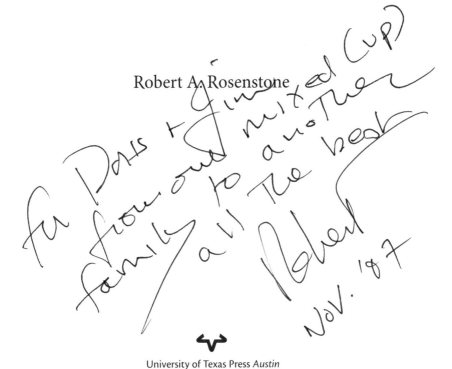

The (Mostly) True Story of My Jewish Family

Robert A. Rosenstone

University of Texas Press *Austin*

This book has been supported by The Jewish History, Life, and Culture Series endowment funded by Milton T. and Helen G. Smith and the Moshana Foundation, and the Tocker Foundation.

Requests for permission to reproduce material
from this work should be sent to:

Permissions
University of Texas Press
P.O. Box 7819
Austin, TX 78713-7819

www.utexas.edu/utpress/about/bpermission.html

∞ The paper used in this book meets the minimum requirements
of ANSI/NISO Z39.48-1992 (R1997) (Permanence of Paper).

LIBRARY OF CONGRESS CATALOGING-IN-PUBLICATION DATA

Rosenstone, Robert A.
The man who swam into history : the (mostly) true story of my Jewish family /
Robert A. Rosenstone.— 1st University of Texas Press ed.
p.   cm. — (Jewish history, life, and culture)
ISBN 0-292-70950-1 (pbk. : alk. paper)
1. Rosenstone family.   2. Jews—Romania—Moldavia—Biography.   3. Jews,
Romanian—Québec (Province)—Montréal—Biography.   4. Jews, Canadian—
California—Biography.   5. Moldavia (Romania)—Biography.   6. Montréal
(Québec)—Biography.   7. California—Biography.   I. Title.   II. Series.
DS135.R73R677   2005
929'.2'089924071—dc22
2005005621

In Loving Memory—for Hannah and Lazar

Contents

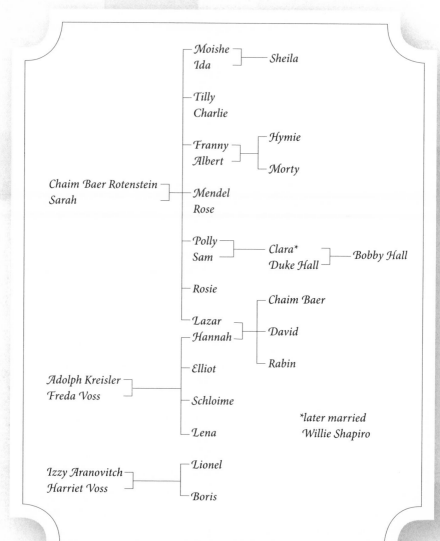

Chaim Baer Rotenstein
Sarah

- Moishe
  Ida — Sheila

- Tilly
  Charlie

- Franny
  Albert — Hymie
          — Morty

- Mendel
  Rose

- Polly
  Sam — Clara*
        Duke Hall — Bobby Hall

- Rosie

- Lazar
  Hannah — Chaim Baer
           — David
           — Rabin

Adolph Kreisler
Freda Voss

- Elliot

- Schloime

- Lena

*later married
Willie Shapiro

Izzy Aranovitch
Harriet Voss

- Lionel

- Boris

Introduction

On the morning of May 9, 1997, a day I was scheduled to deliver an evening lecture to the British Academy entitled *Looking at the Past in a Postliterate Age, or Is Oliver Stone a Historian?*, I decided to visit the synagogue in which my maternal grandparents had been married ninety-five years before. My reasons for doing so were at once sentimental and instrumental. The manuscript of the work you now hold in your hands was almost complete, but I was searching for an introduction that would hold together this collection about my family. A visit to the synagogue held out a vague promise: I would touch the past, see what my grandparents had seen, perhaps feel what they felt, and the result would be one of those moments that leads to insight and creativity—and, I hoped, to an introduction.

The telephone directory did not list a Stepney Green synagogue. A helpful woman who answered the telephone at the social service agency, Jewish Meals on Wheels, explained why. A decade earlier it had closed because there were not enough Jews in the neighborhood to make a congregation, but the building was still standing and one could at least view it from the outside. Following her detailed directions, my wife and I left the Stepney Green tube station in the East End and were confronted with a sense both of historical continuity and irony: as in my grandparents' day, this was still a neighborhood of immigrants, only now the majority were obviously Muslim—dark-skinned men, some of them in djellabas, carrying worry beads; women with scarves over their heads, a few completely covered from head to toe in flowing chadours.

The synagogue was neither tiny, as I had imagined fitting for my impoverished forebears, nor empty. In front of us stood an imposing four-story structure surrounded by the temporary fence of a building site, its walls masked by scaffolding. Through the large, arched main door, workmen carried wallboard, wiring, paint buckets and brushes, loads of lumber, and copper pipes. The explanation came from a gray-haired man who introduced himself as The Builder. The synagogue was being renovated, cut into apartments. A shame, yes, but it was the only way of saving the structure from being vandalized. As a Registered Building, nothing major could be altered. The stained glass, the abstract mosaics, the biblical quotations in Hebrew and English in the main hallway and within the apartments—all this would remain. Taking a shower you might comfort yourself with words from Leviticus.

The hour I spent there snapping photos, stumbling over wires, slipping on wet spots, sticking my elbow into fresh paint, and ducking workers carrying tools and building materials did not add up to my imagined period of quiet contemplation. But we have to take our metaphors where we can find them. To save the synagogue, they had to alter the structure, change it, fragment it into spaces that had little or nothing to do with the original purposes of the building or the ceremonies that had taken place there during its century as a religious center. To save the synagogue, they had to hide away some things, subtract others, highlight still others. Gone was the carved wooden balcony from which the women had looked down on the services; gone was the altar and the niche for the sacred scrolls. The pillars that once stood free now rose through kitchens and living rooms; the circular stained glass just beneath the ceiling and the tablets with the Ten Commandments that may have been lost in the broad vistas of the original structure were now the focal point of the three-story open central hallway.

Stepney Green Synagogue was, in short, like any work of history. To save the past—as biographer, autobiographer, memoirist, or historian—we translate the remaining traces of it into language and forms of writing which necessarily alter and fragment things, highlight some moments and erase others. In writing history we describe and interpret moments and events which participants experienced and interpreted in far different ways. This is to say that, as with the synagogue, we are always altering the remains of the past for our own needs in the present. With words (or images, or sounds) we attempt to simulate a lost world, but the life we bestow upon the dead is not one they would recognize as their own.

The origins of this book lie in a single sentence that more than a decade ago entered my mind one morning when I was jogging on the beach: *There is a man who comes swimming into history.* That man, my father's father, had died thirty years before my own birth. All I knew about him was that single fact, presented in family lore as unique and heroic, a mark of the rare qualities of our lineage. My grandfather had swum the roaring and dangerous Prut River to get to Romania and escape the military draft in Russia. Only later did I learn that almost every grandfather of every Jewish Romanian claimed the same athletic feat.

When the sentence came to me, I was already a professor of history who was in that dangerous period called midlife. The two major books I had so far published and the third that I was then completing were works that stressed biography rather than the more impersonal forces of history such as social class, nationalism, economic development, or technological change—all of which never seem quite as real to me as people's lives. For two decades my research had focused on marginal characters, people torn between two cultures—American bohemians and radicals of the early twentieth century (*Romantic Revolutionary: A Biography of John Reed*), Communists of the 1930s and 1940s (*Crusade of the Left: The Lincoln Battalion in the Spanish Civil War*), and American sojourners in late-nineteenth-century Japan (*Mirror in the Shrine: American Encounters with Meiji Japan*). I had always believed these topics had arisen largely from personal experiences—college newspaper editor campaigning against racial discrimination in the 1950s, would-be novelist living in the Latin Quarter, graduate student supporting the Free Speech Movement, activist in the Mobilization against the Vietnam War, professor teaching American studies at Kyushu University in Japan. It never occurred to me that my choices might also connect to my heritage. That if you are born into an immigrant family with parents from two cultures as different and conflicting in values as those of Latvia and Romania (the German and the Latin), a family in which racketeers and Communists and extramarital love affairs were unremarkable, you might have a tendency to take an interest in characters torn between the values and beliefs of different worlds.

Like many children of immigrants of that era, I had (unconsciously) spent a good part of my life becoming an American. In the fifties, when I went to high school and college, this meant adapting to a certain kind of speech and dress, and a certain set of values. For someone born in Canada, this was easy. My parents might sound and look as if their origins lay in some other continent, but not me. And yet at the same time, in school I was always plagued (unconsciously) by the need to prove something—something that must have had to do, though I would never consciously feel this, with being the child of Jewish immigrants. This meant believing and acting differently from those social leaders who belonged to clubs, fraternities, and sororities. It meant taking to heart the core ideals of America—freedom, equality, and justice for all—and attempting to make sure that people and political leaders lived up to them.

This desire to be the same and yet different seems to have emerged in many of my academic and personal choices. Undergraduate major: English, with a focus on American literature. Graduate major: American history. First wife: American lineage back to the seventeenth century. Topics for books: John Reed, the quintessential wasp radical, the Harvard man who becomes the golden boy of bohemia, then chronicles the Mexican and Bolshevik revolutions, founds the Communist Party, and ends up buried in the Kremlin wall; those nineteenth-century sojourners in Japan, mostly New Englanders who are intent upon carrying the values of Christianity and Western civilization to the natives, but who stay long enough to learn the natives are quite civilized already. Even my work on the International Brigades in Spain did not deal with the volunteers as Jews, which so many were, but focused (as did the Lincoln Brigaders themselves) on the struggle to defend the traditional values of Western civilization: democracy, republicanism, free speech, the secular state.

Midlife is a time of reckoning. My parents were rapidly aging, my father having the heart attacks and strokes that would lead eventually to an institution, my mother experiencing the first bouts of forgetfulness—not yet named Alzheimer's—that would make her unable to speak anything other than poetic gibberish. Part of the reckoning is a growing self-consciousness, one that for this professional historian raised the question: how do I fit into History, the history I live as opposed to the one I chronicle. The question obviously extends to include one's family, even if they don't wish to be included. Like so many immigrants of their generation, my mother and father never wanted to talk about the Old Country and I, self-centered young (naturalized) American, had never been interested enough to raise the issue. Now in my mid-forties, as their lives become more important to me, I began to press them to talk about their childhoods, their own parents, their memories of schools, journeys, occupations, other relatives, family events.

The shards of memory, the moments and tales shared by my parents and then by other family members over the next decade eventually grew into this book. (Some were already there, in my consciousness, long before I knew I was hearing them or interested in what they were.) The words with which I evoke the past are a mixture of their voices and other voices that began to speak in my head—sometimes in the first person, sometimes in the second, sometimes in the third. For years I attempted to turn them into one coherent, unified voice, to smooth the narrative, but when I tried to do so, they stopped speaking. The result is a story told from a variety of points of view and in a variety of styles, a book of tales, sequences, windows, moments, and fragments resurrected from the lives of three generations in my two parental families, set in five countries on two continents over the period of almost a century. Each segment of the work can, I think, stand on its own, though taken together they suggest a larger story.

Putting together these pieces, I felt it unnecessary to tell yet another complete immigrant family saga, because by now we know that story all too well: how poor foreigners, spat upon and reviled, overcame horrendous obstacles to become good Americans. The tale of my family—of every immigrant family—is a story that has already been written. My aim here is to do no more than to seize and render certain moments and experiences that can provide a different perspective on that larger familiar story. In its mixture of genres and styles, this work lies somewhere between history, memoir, and autobiography—the multivoiced story of a lineage that includes (as any such work must) the life of the teller of the tale. It begins with my grandparents and concludes with yours truly in college, at an age when the great family secrets—racketeers on one side, Communists on the other, love affairs on both—are at last revealed. Each section focuses on one or two characters, trying to locate and capture an event or an action or a relationship that defines a larger sense of life's possibilities and meanings. The same characters reappear in other sections, with the result that the work is perhaps closer in form to a collage or a mosaic than to a linear narrative. The narrator of the work tells his tale sometimes in the first person and sometimes in the third: he is Rabin, the historian; he is yours truly; he is the all-seeing I.

Family stories are fashionable these days. A sign of the times, a signal that History may be returning to its roots in history, that we—historians and nonacademics alike—are interested in the world of large events only as they have had an impact upon our own small lives and helped to shape us. Once upon a time, family stories were tales of rags to riches. More recently they have become woeful accounts of abuse and victimization. The themes of any work, as any historian knows, depend less on the subject matter than on the way you tell the story, less upon the events than on your attitude toward them. Struggle, triumph, and victimization, rags and riches, are all part of my family, but what interests me are the moments of daily life, the memories and secrets by which we mark our days, the quirks, oddities, pains, and joys of simple survival; how people, whatever their circumstances, make choices that change their lives and then have to live with the consequences of those choices.

Any work like this is in part based on time spent in archives and libraries, in homes and garages, poring over diaries, letters, photos, newspaper clippings and other stuff pasted into family albums, and on lengthy interviews with sometimes recalcitrant and often forgetful relatives. To give the reader a taste of the kind of sources used and the ways in which I have attempted to use them, one document and one photo are included in each chapter. Such sources are necessary but not sufficient to evoke the past. Anyone who has done historical research knows that it takes more than access to documents to create a truthful or meaningful past. The reality of the past—national, familial, personal—does not lie in an assemblage of data but in a field of stories—a place where fact, truth, fiction, invention, forgetting, and myth are so entangled that they cannot be separated. Ultimately it is not the facts that make us what we are, but the stories we have been told and the stories we believe.

The Man Who Swam *into* History

The author and his parents, Hannah and Lazar, circa 1937, about the time he began to be taken to Moishe's Steak House—even if he couldn't yet eat the steaks.

Romania, Rumania, Roumania

In the early 1940s there was a restaurant in Montreal where the only record in the jukebox was a song named *Romania*. At least it was the only record that could be heard on those crowded Sunday nights when, even with wartime gas rationing, it was difficult to find a parking place on the side streets off of the Main near the basement bagel factory where men worked stripped to the waist and the flavor of the bagels seemed to have something to do with the quality of sweat rolling down their glistening bodies. The restaurant was named Moishe's. It was reached up a long, dark, steep, and evil-smelling flight of stairs that frightened a small child as he climbed to the second floor, where hordes of people bumped and pushed and where, if you were not a Romanian who had known Moishe for a long time, and preferably during days in the Old Country, you might have to wait forever to get a table. The dinner was always the same—steaks much too thick to be anything but black market and much too delicious to be kosher, and marvelously soggy, oily french fried potatoes. But the best dish, even to a child, came first—Moishe's special platter of chopped liver and thin, crisp, fried onions, which you mashed together, salted generously, and devoured in an instant.

The dining room had a tiny wooden dance floor, unused because the ill-lit room was always too jammed with waiters and table-hopping customers. Besides, how could you dance to a song named *Romania*? It was such a sad and serious song that it always made you want to laugh. A male voice began by shrieking, *Romania, Romania, Romania, Romania, Romania,* then it drooped into sobbing, *Romania, Romania, Romania, Romania,* then it lilted away into mellower tears, *Romania, Romania, Romania…* until you could not hear it any more because the restaurant was far too noisy. In an occasional rare moment, when the din lessened, a word that was not *Romania* might enter through one small ear into consciousness. If you asked an adult who had been born in that country what was being said, the answer was always definitive: *It's about Romania.*

There was something profound about exposure to Moishe's jukebox. Take a child on wartime Sunday nights when hunger has made his stomach and brain equally susceptible to outside influence, and you may mark him for life. Hearing *Romania* year in, year out in that setting leaves you with a feeling that can never be shaken or altered by later facts or experiences: namely that there was and is and always will be something inherently odd, off-kilter, lopsided, humorous, warped, untidy, even ridiculous about Romania. Later information only confirms this attitude. The spelling, for instance. Nobody, least of all anyone who had actually lived there, could ever tell a bright child if it was *Rumania* or *Romania* or *Roumania,* and if you became insistent they either said *Who cares?* or told you to go chop a teakettle. Or the history. Was Carol a name proper for a king? And what was his queen's name, then—George? (Very funny among nine-year-olds waiting at Moishe's.) College history courses only made it worse. In any other country did military officers wear corsets and rouge and just a touch of pale lipstick, darling?

One long-range result is this: You can stand before Trajan's Column in Rome, ignore the tabby cats cringing beneath crumbling brick walls, the water leaking through a hole in your umbrella and coldly trickling down your neck, your wet woolen socks and fears that you won't be able to find enough vitamin C in the Eternal City to cure the eternal cold that is about to descend with all the ferocity of ancient legionnaires; you can stand outside the iron picket fence while Fiats and Alfa Romeos squish past, and like Gibbon brood over the immense symbolic questions raised by a structure that has been standing erect for almost two millennia. But later, leafing through an art book, when you see close-ups of the frieze winding upward around the column and learn that the story carved into rock tells of Trajan's greatest triumph, the conquest of the Dacians, these nobles in odd-looking, brimless hats, unknowing and no doubt unwilling ancestors of modern Romanians, somehow the column begins to shrink, dwindle, diminish in the winter rain. The next time in Rome you visit the Arch of Titus, with its frieze recording that emperor's triumphant victory over the King of Judah.

The Rotenstein family house in Tetscani, taken by Chaim Baer's eldest son, Moishe, in the mid-1960s. He was the only family member rich and/or crazy enough to make a trip back to Romania.

The Man Who Swam

The Jews, who are to be found in all Rumanian provinces and have big communities in Bessarabia and the Bukovina, have always been a persecuted and oppressed minority. The brand of anti-Semitism encouraged by almost all Rumanian governments resembles that of Tsarist Russia. Whenever something went wrong in politics or economics the Jews were blamed for it and pogroms were organized, sometimes surpassing in violence those of the Tsarist regime. This traditional anti-Semitism has its roots in the period when wealthy Rumanian absentee landlords let their estates to Jewish agents for management and tax-collection. This was a convenient means of laying the blame for exploitation at the door of the Jews, whilst the boiars pocketed the taxes and rents. Jewish influence in Rumanian finance and trade has been very great, as was their share in introducing modern industries into the country. Many Jewish families, especially in Moldavia and Wallachia, can trace their association with Rumania back to the early Phanariots. Others have lived for many years in the Bukovina, in Bessarabia in the Transylvania. The majority has, however, immigrated during the last century. Restrictions on their personal freedom, an almost complete denial of political rights, and organized and government-sponsored pogroms are familiar devices which have been used by most Rumanian regimes. These measures are supported by the ruling circles and certain intellectuals in order to divert the attention of the people from the real causes and the real culprits whenever the country passes through a crisis.

FROM *RUMANIA* BY C. KORMOS

There is a man who comes swimming into history. He first appears in the water of the Prut River during the last quarter of the nineteenth century. The exact date is impossible to determine, but it is in the late Victorian period, though he knows nothing about that sort of label. Before he plunges headlong into the waters, or gingerly steps into the waters, there is little to know about him, little that can ever be discovered. He kept no diary and told no tales that his children would ever remember. The waters of the river cleansed him, washed away his past. Like some version of the Venus myth, he arises naked and full grown, innocent of history. His wisdom, if any, is water wisdom, the wisdom of currents and sea foam. He is not quite self-made, but he is more than the creation of some god's imagination.

For twenty-five, perhaps thirty years, the man-who-swims-into-history lives in Moldavia. His tongue, trained to the disparate sounds of Yiddish, Russian, and Hebrew, can never quite adjust to the soft Latin vocal of the native language. The wife he acquires is fluent in Polish. Their children, the three boys and four girls who live to maturity, grow up speaking Romanian. If he must communicate with natives through a heavy accent and an impoverished vocabulary, it does not matter; even in the Yiddish shared with the family, he has little to say. There may be words in him, but they are not the kind spoken with the mouth. They are voiced with the language of the body, the bowels, the eyes.

His means of communication are the scissors and sewing machine, part of a language that also crossed the river. He is a skilled tailor, far different from most small-town practitioners who patch together the threadbare remnants of worried lives. His hands, capable of creating new suits, know the feel of fine cloth, woven in far-off British mills; they understand that the cut of a jacket, drape of a coat, turn of a lapel, and angled fall of trousers make even a poor man feel, on the day of a wedding, bar mitzvah, or other holiness, like a king. In any religious theory, a man should not take pride in the ephemera of outward appearance. But his hands know the wisdom of this world, the instinctive blessing that exists outside the pages of any sacred text.

Life in Romania all those years is quiet, regular, tuned to an unvarying pattern of seasons, holidays. Flights of birds, the sowing of corn, clouds rumbling into rain, the annual festival of grapes, the visit of Gypsies—year after year. The man who swims into history fits into the cycle. He is quiet too, perhaps timid. His only vice is gambling. Never is he known to question the customs and laws that circumscribe his days. He takes part in the ceremonies of the small Jewish community of his town, but never with much enthusiasm or faith. His children never see him as angry, upset, or authoritarian, but they do feel his emotional wires are somehow crossed. When it is time to discipline a youngster, he smiles sheepishly and disappears, leaving the task to the strong forearm of his wife. In moments of tragedy or death, he unaccountably grins, sometimes breaks into soft laughter. Then, as if ashamed at the response, he vanishes from the house.

After the swim, he never travels much. Business can take him to the regional center of Bacau, but there is no evidence he ever visits the former Moldavian capital, Iasi, or journeys to Bucharest, less than two hundred miles away. His decision at the turn of the century to leave for America is as much of a surprise to the family as to neighbors. He goes by boat, no doubt from the port of Constanza into the Black Sea. The view from steerage is not very good. A glimpse of domes and minarets, draped across Constantinople's seven hills, or of the massive rock that preserved the Mediterranean for the British sovereign. His voyage consists mainly of dark water, dark bulkheads, dark food, and the dark breath of fellow passengers. At Ellis Island he is turned away, either because he does not have enough money (the version told by his first son, Moishe) or because he is mistaken for an anarchist or some other radical with the same name (the version told by his second son, Lazar). A ship drops him in a French port, and for a year he lives and works in Paris. Rarely does he write letters home. Perhaps he doesn't know how to write.

Some years later there is money for the whole family to go. Lazar will remember but a single incident from the trip. Passing on a train or in a streetcar, or stopped in station in either France or England, the family is assaulted with the violent, incomprehensible words of street urchins, who hurl clods of dung along with insults. The future becomes a lottery spun by some god of the shipping lines and lanes. Their money gone, the family decides to take the next ship out, whether it goes to Canada or to Argentina. They land in a city buried in white snowbanks higher than the tallest midteen child. By the time the sky melts into blue and bright flowers spring out all over the mountain that rises in the middle of the island of Montreal, home is a dim apartment off the Main. Mother is, as always, in the kitchen much of the time, but the children have no garden to tend, no chickens or goats to feed, no cow to milk. The boys scatter into the streets, and the sounds of English become familiar in their mouths. The girls feel a sweet tender swelling as they hang by the iron stairways that curve gracefully from second-story duplexes to the sidewalk. They look past their brothers to catch the eyes of other men.

The man-who-swims-into-history remains silent. He speaks neither of Russia, Romania, or the New World, says nothing about past or future, never discusses the Prut River, the Black Sea, the Atlantic Ocean, the Seine, or the St. Lawrence. In the garment factory where he works with many other men whose language he cannot understand, his hands seem less graceful, agile, expressive than before. It is tempting to believe that in this silence he is preparing a message for his children, and the grandchildren and great-grandchildren of all immigrants. Such words cannot come easily or quickly. First there is the matter of a lump on his head, an old companion that has made every journey with him. The operation is routine. Less than a year after arriving in Canada, he leaves his family for a single night in a huge, modern hospital of a kind none of them had seen in Romania. Once the lump has been removed and a bandage wrapped tightly around his head, he never seems quite well. At home and work he is dizzy, vague, tired. A few days after the surgery he returns from the shop, goes to bed, and never gets up again. With the family gathered around, his last words are simple: *Take care of your mother.* Then the man-who-swims-into-history floats out of history without leaving any message for his descendants. Perhaps we must look for any message back there in the waters of the Prut, in the Black Sea and the Mediterranean, in the storms of the English Channel and the hurricanes that sweep the Atlantic seaboard, in breakers off the coast of California and typhoons that slam out of the South Pacific onto the islands of Japan. For a man who swims into it, history must exist in water or not at all.

···———

His name was Chaim Baer and he was walking. The roads were dusty, the day hot. There were vineyards and cornfields. The towns were small, wooden, sagging, each with a church, implacable, arrogant, alien. This is what he would be leaving. He would be leaving nothing. Less than nothing. Family. Yes, family. But the family was not his, was not him. There was a tie, but there was not a tie, and there were no words to explain this. He did not belong to anyone. Maybe not even himself. The road felt good underfoot. Each step was taking him somewhere. Going somewhere, this is what he had wanted for a long time. Being on a road, going past blue vineyards, feeling the summer sun hot on the back of his neck, feeling the dust of travel, knowing there was somewhere else. He had a feeling that there was somewhere else. But when he tried to share it with friends, they could not understand. Looking down to the harbor, the gray bulk of ships from all over the world, most people turned their eyes to home. They did not want to see where the ships came from. They did not understand his itch to move. If he did not belong here, he did not belong anywhere. He did not belong anywhere. Right now he belonged to the road, to his legs beginning to ache and his dusty shoes, to the pain in his neck from the pack slung at an angle across his shoulder, to the sagging wooden villages, the crippled dogs hiding in the shade of drooping porches, the blank-eyed peasants staring through him, and the churches, always the churches, dark and ramshackle or sunny white, straight lines soaring toward heaven, topped with a golden onion dome.

Arrogant towers, arrogant gold. And always next to graveyards where we cannot be buried. Nor they in ours, and who would want them? These churches, this soil, the dust of the graveyard, the crumbling crosses. Not ours, never could be ours. Decrees stamped by the czar, his ministers, locked away in St. Petersburg's tomblike vaults. And if we could make it ours, it would be no use. It would be a game, a deception. Then we would be like them. The land is not to own. It is not ours. Not theirs. It's His. Yet He probably does not exist. Or does He look down and laugh when I think that? Let Him laugh. If He's such a big shot He'd let us know about Him, let us see sometimes. Why does He speak in books, why must we learn to read to understand His words? That's to keep jobs for the rabbis, smart types all their lives with eyes white on the pages of a book.

Chaim Baer put his hand to his face, touched the newly smooth cheeks, the one tuft of hair sprouting from the chin. It is like being a boy again, a bar mitzvah boy with this smoothness. His hair shows the joke of life. Red, a tiny red beard on the chin. Everyone will notice and comment on the contrast from my dark hair. Young ladies, won't they be interested? They'll think I am one of them, maybe, a red beard and these blue eyes. Strange eyes, my mother said, the eyes of my father. Such a strange story. In each generation, one male in the family with blue eyes. Is it a special sign? Or sometime in the past did a muzhik or a strange tribesman lie with a woman in the family? A horseback warrior would be better. On a horse you are always going somewhere. On foot I am going somewhere, only it takes longer.

The road goes on through nights and days. Blanket roll in a cornfield, beneath a moon asking questions that are not answered by the stars. Moving toward a horizon, one step at a time through dust of hot afternoons. Gulp cold water at a stream, sneak from the road to pick grapes, snatch unripe corn and gobble it uncooked, raw white. At twilight, frogs sing in ditches; at night, crickets; in the pale hours before dawn, birds whose names he did not know. Sometimes the thought: this has been done before. I am doing it, me walking, but it is someone else with blue eyes and a red goatee. It is a strange feeling, standing by the side of a road in a dust cloud raised by an ox-pulled cart, choking a little, tickling in the nose, to know it is someone else standing there, holding a finger to the nose to keep from sneezing. At night in a bedroll in a vineyard, crickets cheering the moon higher into the sky, you feel you are not alone. He knew this had been done before. He knew it would be done again. On foot, on horseback, on a riverboat. Some other way that was no different, always the same. In each generation there was one son with blue eyes. In each generation there was one son with an itch. It had to be someone on horseback, from Central Asia or the lands beyond. One pair of blue eyes, one horse, and one itch. That was the thought he held on to every night when the moon sang him to sleep.

$$\cdots =\!\!=\!\!=\!\!=$$

It is a little-noted fact of history that the rivers of Eastern Europe were jammed with swimmers in the last quarter of the nineteenth century. Not one grandfather but a whole generation of grandfathers sidling, walking, waddling, hurrying, moseying, lurching, striding, flinging, leaping, jumping, tiptoeing, plunging, screaming themselves into previously empty waters. They were not yet grandfathers, but somehow the image is of aged men, dressed fully in black, yarmulkes affixed firmly to their scalps, long white beards floating miraculously and gently on the surface as they flash toward far-off shores. Are they not praying as they swim, shawls around their shoulders, voices raised to the Lord to drown the fearful beating of their hearts. In later years, none of these grandfathers were ever known to go near the water. None ever could teach his sons how to swim, any more than they could teach them how to play baseball, steal a bagel, or make love to a woman, all skills apparently more necessary in the New World than in the Old. Decades later they were full of foolish tales, babbled in languages that grandsons neither understood nor cared much about. But each grandfather had this one moment of undisputed triumph that would quietly resonate through future generations.

$$\cdots =\!\!=\!\!=\!\!=$$

Romania, Rumania, Roumania—but what is Romania? Modern historians of the late, unlamented People's Republic of Romania seemed unclear about the nature of their country. When leading scholars in 1970 issued a multiauthored work as part of a national History Series, they entitled it *Istoria Popurului Roman*, which translates as *History of the Romanian People* and suggests that the nation itself may be a figment of somebody's imagination. Numerous peoples are mentioned in the more than six hundred pages of the book—Scythians, Avars, Ionians, Dorians, Dacians, Geto-Dacians, Cimmerians, Thracians, Celts, Bastarnians, Samatians, Goths, Visigoths, Ostrogoths, Bulgars, Huns, and Pechenegs. Jews (Hebrews) receive but a few passing nods. Nowhere does this work mention that close to a million descendants of the children of Israel once lived within the borders of modern Romania or that they constituted 5 percent of the population and a social problem that turned the head of more than a single statesman gray.

Romania in the late nineteenth century was a new name for an old idea, one linked to three provinces, but Transylvania, with its tales of vampires and population of Hungarians, did not count for much. The two other regions, Moldavia and Walachia, had for four hundred years been part of that geographic sprawl known as the Ottoman Empire. In Constantinople the sultans had come to prefer opium, sweets, and belly dancers to running a government, and who could blame them? Rather than bother with the insoluble problems assailing infidel peasants, they in the late eighteenth century began to subcontract the governing of these dreary provinces to clever Greek merchants who lived in the Phanar district of Constantinople. Greeks were infidels too, but infidels capable of coming up with large sums of gold, which proved useful in satisfying the rulers' unceasing appetite for young girls, sought all over the sultan's domains, which stretched from the Atlantic Coast of Africa to the eastern boundary of the Anatolian Plateau.

Greek merchants cared little about opium, sweets, or belly dancers. Their aesthetic sense responded to the sight of the painted hulls and clean, white sails of vessels from the Mediterranean, Atlantic, and far-off Indian Ocean ports, bobbing in the murky waters of the Golden Horn, and their religious impulse was fulfilled by the satisfying clatter of coins across a polished counter. Moldavia and Walachia might contain endless, dismal collections of hovels, swimming in seas of mud, and be found somewhere at the far end of the universe, but there was no shortage of volunteers to govern them. Each ruler—they called themselves *Phanariot Princes,* but everyone knew they were only Greeks—arrived at his new post burdened by two problems: one was the vast debt incurred in buying the throne; the other, the knowledge that a more affluent merchant might quickly buy it out from under him.

Greeks seeking gifts proved more than equal to the task. As they liked to point out, their ancestors had, after all, invented democratic government more than two thousand years before. This, apparently, is what allowed them to use the public treasury to pay nonexistent workers to build mythical public works. Or to forbid certain imports, then put smugglers on the payroll and open stores to fence their goods. Or to sell administrative, judicial, and ecclesiastical offices to the highest bidder, and to appropriate church revenues for themselves, perhaps to keep temptation from being placed before the eyes of those who serve the Lord. When peasants began to burn their own houses and slaughter their sheep and cattle to avoid the property and the livestock taxes, the princes seized the furniture and livestock. Actions like this are bound to leave scar tissue on a national psyche. Historians agree that Phanariot rule had an effect on future Romanian social, political, and cultural institutions. But historians are a cautious, unimaginative lot, unwilling to specify exactly what such effects were. So here is one suggestion: in the 1940s in Montreal the first joke that any Romanian man told his eldest son was the following:

Do you know how to make a Romanian omelette?

No.

First you steal two eggs…

By the time Chaim Baer drags soggily onto the Moldavian shore of the Prut, Phanariot princes have long vanished and the Turkish sultan himself no longer exercises authority over the region. Since the early nineteenth century the Balkans had been boiling with independence movements and bloody uprisings. Troops of czars named Nicholas and Alexander had fought victorious battles against the Ottomans, an entire Russian army had taken a six-year vacation in Bucharest, six hundred nearsighted British cavalrymen had swept to a glorious death at Balaklava, and statesmen in frock coats and whiskers had conferred in Paris, signed treaties in Berlin. There were two major results of all this. One was an independent Romania. The other was the necessity for Chaim Baer's grandson, Rabin, as a fourth-grade student in Montreal, to learn by heart a poem beginning *Half a league, half a league, half a league onward.*

Romania was not only an independent nation, it was also a kingdom. But the king was not Romanian. No Romanian was qualified for such a job. In truth, the king did not even speak Romanian, but his German was excellent and his French not bad. His name was Charles of Hohenzollern-Sigmaringen (the locals called him King Carol), and he was selected in a plebiscite by an official margin of 685,969 to 224. Because Carol was a Prussian, the Hapsburgs of Austria-Hungary were not much impressed with his credentials and more than a little suspicious over the lopsided results of the election. Someone in the entourage of Emperor Franz Joseph spread rumors in European court circles that the new ruler would be arrested by Austrian police on the way to his coronation. Carol was undeterred; he was a Hohenzollern after all. He traveled through Austria-Hungary carrying the heavy bags of a traveling salesman and wearing bright blue goggles, took a second-class cabin on a Danube steamer out of Vienna, and arrived safely in his new hometown. A slight hernia was a small price to pay to become king of the Dacians.

The king might never learn to speak the native tongue, but the citizens of his land were touchy about their prerogatives and, as people who claimed descent from Roman legions, inordinately proud of their heritage. Scratch a Romanian and he was sure to point how his unique ancestry, so different from his rude Slav, Bulgar, and Magyar neighbors, made him fit to run an empire. How appalling it was to learn that at the Congress of Berlin in 1878, which guaranteed Rumanian independence, the Great Powers insisted on a treaty article requiring Roumania to return to her Jewish residents the civil rights that had been denied them in the 1866 constitution. Manfully, eloquently, passionately, the leaders of the new nation fought the proposal. It was a crime, they said, to deny the sovereign right of a nation with such a glorious heritage to persecute, disfranchise, and otherwise abuse some (or, for that matter, all) of its residents. Such arguments fell on deaf ears. The solemn will of Prussia, Austria-Hungary, France, and Great Britain prevailed. At least on paper.

Between the southern bank of the Prut and the Moldavian village of Tetscani there is a blank, more of time than space. Chaim Baer acquires a wife, a business, a house, a vegetable garden, a cow, then a second cow. Seven children arrive, bracketed by the considerable number of stillbirths and miscarriages that were normal for that era, that region of the world. Life might be as routine as in any peasant community, but for the diversion thoughtfully provided by the government. It is the mayor who comes to the house to explain. Chaim Baer offers him a cup of tea, listens quietly, patiently, nodding his head. The mayor is a fellow card-player. He has no desire to perform his official duty, but it is not his fault that the time has come for Chaim Baer's family to leave Tetscani. When the teacups are empty, the two men stand up, shake hands, part. There are no harsh words, no regrets, no deep sadness. Each understands that life is what life is.

The family loads its possessions in a cart and leaves Tetscani for Moinesti, some kilometers away. A few months, or a year or two later, they make the same journey in the opposite direction. These periodic moves partake of a mystery. Official government policy prevents Jews from becoming citizens and from owning land. But nothing is said in historical studies, constitutions, available decrees and statutes to indicate that there is a time limit on Jews residing in small towns or rural areas. Was it officially unofficial, carefully concealed from European statesmen, not even committed to paper so that foreign politicians with special constituencies or certain banking houses that might be persuaded to invest in Romanian development would not know? Was it local custom in Moldavia, sanctioned by decades or centuries of repetition? To Chaim Baer, his wife, and their children, reasons would have made little difference. The upset and confusion of packing, hauling, setting up in Moinesti were an unsought diversion. There is evidence enough that Chaim Baer was the sort of man who understood the spiritual benefits of an occasional change of scenery.

For Chaim Baer's children, Romania would always be Tetscani. Moinesti is a dim memory, fragments of cobblestones, tall two- and three-story buildings, crowds in paved streets, butcher shops where the boys worked briefly. Tetscani was where life became real, but only the occasional event or fragment of daily life would remain in the minds of Chaim Baer's children half a century later. These moments throw an unusual light over Tetscani. We imagine the color of Eastern Europe to be brown, the sepia tones of picture books on suburban coffee tables in the last third of the twentieth century. Tetscani is saturated with raw color: green of corn glowing in the summer sun, hillsides speckled with bright wildflowers, the purple feet of children and adults after a dance on the grapes, white bodies in ice-green streams where youngsters learn how to swim. The shtetl is dun faces full of suffering, acceptance, pain, wonder; invisible bodies clad in coats, hats, dresses long and weighty, dark and confining, personal prisons that reinforce a mentality, a way of life. Tetscani has no rabbis in black; no pale, stooped yeshiva students; no bulky synagogue brooding over the community. Weekly services for the six Jewish families take place in a room behind a store. Religion is quiet, humble, personal, a time for talking directly to Him or meditating softly on His absence.

Days, months, years vanish quickly behind the wispy membrane of consciousness we call the universe. Chaim Baer works at the sewing machine; the children milk the cows and tend the garden; his wife, Sarah, bakes fresh bread in a wood-burning oven and covers her eyes when she lights candles every Friday night at sundown. Saturday, after the Sabbath ends, is the time for indulgence. Chaim Baer loves the noisy camaraderie of the gaming table, where religion and faith ride heavily on the size of a bet, the chance turn of a card. Summer days may find him spending afternoons with his youngsters, seven of them tumbling along cornfield rows, climbing into hilly vineyards surrounding the gray-walled estates of local nobles. In the autumn everyone—peasants, townspeople, relatives from far off, even Jews—are welcome in the fields and courtyards of the stone chateau owned by the Rossetti family. Everyone helps to haul grapes, lift them into barrels, stomp them with clean feet, then gather amidst pigs and chickens at long trestle tables in the courtyard to sing songs, drink the fresh juice and sample last year's vintage, then roar home, men, women, and children, and before the dry throats and sharp headaches of the morrow, try a quick moment of love where the nimble ankles and firm calves of peasant girls mingle with the slow movements of a heavy body you know too well.

Once a year Gypsies arrive to camp, barter, gamble, entertain, tell fortunes. Like all the children of Tetscani, Chaim Baer's kids hang around the high-wheeled caravans, regarding the visitors with expressions that seem to equate dark skin, cracked teeth, and golden earrings with worlds of wonder. Adults are more cynical. Each year when the nomads depart, villagers complain to each other about all the items, large and small, that have mysteriously vanished from their households. Chaim Baer does not join in such talk. This is no identification of underdogs, no equation of Jew and Gypsy as outsiders. It is temperament. He is not a critical sort, not even of men with rings in their ears who begin by losing and invariably end up winning at any evening of cards they are invited to enter.

There is a good story about Chaim Baer and a Gypsy. The man came to the house one year and wheedled the tailor into letting him try on a half-finished suit. Perhaps he had played cards with Chaim Baer and found him an easy mark. Once clad in the garment, his own clothing lying in a damp heap on the floor of the front room that doubled as a workshop, the Gypsy smiled, announced he would take the suit, and began to walk toward the door without offering to pay. We can imagine Chaim Baer's reaction—if not anger, at least consternation. He must have tried to block the door, so the Gypsy stood there and began to expose the hairy recesses of his body and to pluck, for the tailor's inspection, a few of the tenacious, hardy creatures who resided in them. Politely his visitor explained that of course the suit could not be sold now, for he was prepared to let everyone know that he had worn it. While he talked, the Gypsy cracked lice between his teeth and spat them on the floor like grape seeds. When Chaim Baer absorbed the logic and force of his argument, he stepped away from the door while the Gypsy covered his head with a battered hat, touched his fingers to the brim and vanished.

There is no way of knowing if this incident affected Chaim Baer's behavior, viewpoint, or attitudes toward Gypsies. Every image of him is that of a tolerant, accepting man. Except for the hints of dislike for his wife's sister, but who knows what is lost or gained in the distorting effect of a half-century's distance? She lived in Bucharest and regularly arrived in Tetscani to grace the family with her presence. Rich by marriage to a businessman, her clothing, accent, manners, air, and interests reeked with the scent of city life—with contempt for peasants, land, countryside, cows, and people evidently too dumb or unambitious to live in Bucharest. Chaim Baer's children loved her. The visits were like holidays, a time of excitement, food treats, presents. Ever after they would remember her smell of good soap and perfume, her clothing, the silken dresses that the girls liked to touch; and on her feet, beneath her gowns, thin-soled, immaculate high-heeled shoes unlike anything ever seen before in the muddy roads of Tetscani.

Her arrival meant that Chaim Baer and his wife were forced out of their bedroom. During the days of her visit the sound of female voices jabbering in Polish rode through the hum of the sewing machine. The tailor left the house for solitary walks. Was it only his imagination that his normally docile wife became distracted and testy during such visits, and that this mood hung on for days after her sister's departure? In front of the children his demeanor did not change, but decades later the second son, Lazar, recalled how often Chaim Baer would speak to them with an uncharacteristic mixture of pride and joy of the misfortune that befell their aunt. Her husband had made his money as a building contractor. This was Romania, where every contract was sealed with a payoff that led to another contract. At last he was awarded a huge job that would secure his fortune, one that involved paving the streets of a substantial section of Bucharest. The night before work was to begin, all was ready and in place—piles of sand, rocks, shovels, picks, heaps of necessary tools and equipment. A freak windstorm—hurricane, typhoon, tornado—roared through the city that night, tearing roofs off houses, demolishing shacks, scattering sand, rocks, tools. Chaim Baer's brother-in-law was ruined. His wife never again came to Tetscani. Perhaps they moved to another country. For the children their aunt simply vanished, to be recalled only at certain seasons by scents and memories of the past.

Everyone remembers Chaim Baer as a kind father; some people thought him indulgent to the point of foolishness. The arrival of the first automobile is a good example. News had come through in advance: Danger! Clear the streets! Children were packed into houses, doors were locked, faces peered through curtains as if awaiting a glimpse of doomsday. And there were Chaim Baer and the seven children, crowded together on the tiny front step behind the sagging wooden fence that separated the front yard from the dirt of the main street. No doubt the tailor was more nervous than he admitted. He pulled the children close, held the two babies in his arms. Worries about the wisdom of his actions were underscored by the angry whispers of his wife through the closed front door, demanding he bring at least the infants back inside. Bravado triumphed over common sense. Noise, dust, and a metal contraption with two pale figures blew past. Later they all walked down to the main square. The machine was parked in front of Tetscani's single inn. Adults spoke in hushed tones while the children reached hands out to the shiny, black metal, eyes full of more wonder than Gypsy carts could evoke.

· · · ——

In all stories the children emerge as far more important to Chaim Baer than his wife. This is more than selective memory—it is heritage. The man could not only swim broad rivers and brave speeding machines, he could defy tradition in more fundamental ways. Such as when sickness struck the two eldest boys, a frightening palsy, a nervous disease, a terrible twitching and shaking. They could not sleep or keep food down, and two small bodies were beginning to waste away. The doctor from Moinesti could make no diagnosis. A rabbi promised prayers. Chaim Baer found a peasant woman who practiced either folk medicine or witchcraft. Perhaps he was the first Jew ever to request her services. The remedy was simple: dig into the earth under the bed where the boys slept until you found some coal-like rocks. Grind them into powder, mix with cow's milk and have the boys drink the mixture. Chaim Baer dug. The rocks were there. The mixture was prepared. It looked awful. It tasted awful. The twitching and shaking ended quickly. When sometime later Lazar came down with a very high fever and his mind wandered into delirium, there were no calls for doctors or rabbis. The tailor went directly to the old woman and followed her advice to wrap the youngster in the skin of a pig. For three days the boy sweated and moaned and rolled on his bed and yelled aloud, and on the fourth day he arose, cool and healthy once again.

More than seventy years later, when childhood was far clearer than his morning's breakfast, Lazar would tell his own son this story more than once, wondrously, disbelievingly, incapable of understanding how such a cure had worked, perhaps hoping that another such cure would be brought to him again. After months in modern hospitals, his mind was so blitzed by medical technology that he could no longer understand the truth of his own experience—memory was a legend he could neither accept nor disbelieve.

····───────

Sitting and smelling the ripeness of damp earth and winds blowing before rainstorms. Was there time on afternoons while clouds piled up over the Carpathian Mountains, over the irregular quilt of wheatfields crumpled into foothills, over the limp, brown tassels of cornstalks, the twisted vines where pregnant grapes swelled beneath tight purple skins—was there time to wonder in those hours locked between past and future? Behind pale blue eyes, speaking through them, was a heritage of more than books, the bright impatience of the nomad, a gleam of some tribe that had boiled out of Asia a millennia before. Thoughts came in nouns, without verbs. Restlessness, some unspoken question amidst the noise of swiftly growing children. With surprise, the same surprise that would fill the innocent eyes of his second son almost eighty years later when death still eluded him after strokes, massive heart attacks and pleurisy. Lazar would tell about the brass band parade, led by the pope, that had crashed through the parking lot of Cedars-Sinai Hospital the night before. And the pope, with his golden robes and silver crown, had called up through the sealed window on the sixth floor, called in a powerful voice amplified by no megaphone or loudspeaker, called in fluent Yiddish, *It's time, it's time. Come along, it's time.* Because

Chaim Baer's son was tied to the bed—*poseyed* in the language of hospitals—he was unable to rise, to follow the parade, to follow the pope, and he had to call back, *Next time, maybe next time.* Pain and quick tears scarred the innocence of his eyes as he told the story, then asked, *Do you think they'll return?*

It was the same with Chaim Baer's eyes, waiting for the storms from beyond the mountains, accepting the darkness dropping on Moldavia. Innocent blue eyes had seen it before, fields and churches and rivers, home and friends and parents alter, change, disappear. Sometimes when clouds blew over the mountains, driving down on Tetscani with darkness and wind and the violent slosh of rain, Chaim Baer felt again that strange itch that could not be scratched. There is no reason to believe he had much imagination. In his mind, no images of tropic islands with dusky maidens, of deserts to track, or of empty mountains to climb. No hunger for the delights of bright boulevards, cafés, concert halls, glittering city scenes he could not even picture. Just the noise of rainstorms, that was enough. Trees swaying in gray winds, mud oozing to the ankles, soiling trousers, and a longing in the soles of the feet. Two decades, maybe more—for who could number the years?—since he had swum the Prut. Now one century was ending or another beginning. The difference was the same. It was time to be moving.

Adolph and Freda with their firstborn, taken in London in 1903 or 1904. He has the same blank expression I used to see on his face when he was looking at the stock market reports in the evening paper and muttering to himself. She is wholly unlike the gray-haired grandmother I knew as a child.

TWO

Far from Hasenpoth

There were many fine stores. The Dry Good Stores were really outstand-ing, displaying high class, fine merchandise. There was in midtown a large Apothecary, housed in a very fine building. Next door to the Apo-thecary was a very large building, a club called the Adliger Club, which means royalty, or noblemen. The Barons and Lords from the surround-ing very large estates would come there. There was also a more mod-ern drug store which sold patent medicines and several very fine gro-cery stores. I enjoyed my many walks through the town, filling my eyes with all the sights and sounds of Hasenpoth....

On talking to boys in school and other people, I discovered that Hasenpoth had a population of around five thousand, 50 percent con-sisting of Jews. The non-Jews were mostly of German origin and held themselves superior to the native Latvians, as they had some form of education. The Jews were mostly business people with a sprinkling of artisans such as tailors, shoemakers, wood turners, bakers, cap and hat makers, jewelers and watchmakers. Some of the stores were very well stocked, comparing favorably with those in larger cities.

There were two synagogues, the old and the new. The old one was entirely brick built and stood on a slope, quite a steep hill going down-wards to the River Speeh. The new synagogue was built entirely of stone with a gable. The interior was well fitted out as you see in a modern building today. For lighting it had a number of candelabra, each one for twenty-five candles, which were only lit up on Friday evenings and holidays....

On the side of the new synagogue fronting on Libau St., was the local jail.... The Kirchenberg was beautifully landscaped with flowers and walks.... The church was Lutheran. It was like a park and was used by the townspeople as such. On the Sabbath, I, of course, went with everyone else to the synagogue. On my way to school I would pass a very nice house with two very large trees in front like sentinels. This house was occupied by the Stadt Haupt, the Mayor. Exactly opposite the Mayor's house was a crown school, supported by the Government, but restricted in attendance, especially to Jewish children. A little further on was the house occupied by our school.

Further down the Bayesshe Street was a Russian Church, quite small as there were very few Russian, Greek Orthodox people in Hasenpoth. There was a Russian Priest, an army colonel, a high judge and a custom's inspector, also a coroner. These were the only Russians in town.

Though the language in Hasenpoth was predominantly German, nearly everyone spoke the Latvian tongue. Amongst the Jewish population only German was spoken, however anything of official nature had to be written in Russian because Hasenpoth was in a Russian province.

FROM *THE WAY IT WAS* BY ADOLPH KREISLER

A dolph was not much of a name for a grandfather. At least not in the early 1940s in Montreal. The real Adolph, the one that mattered, was putting people like Grandpa into ovens. Uncles Ziggy and Sammy, for example. Not that anyone ever spoke their names until the phone call that made Mother begin to cry and launched our father, Lazar, into one of his famous stories. The one about how smart he was to cancel those reservations on the *SS Normandie* in August 1939, because he (and apparently he alone) had come to understand right on the eve of sailing that the other Adolph could not be trusted, that there would soon be (drum roll and trumpet flourish) WAR!

Lazar did not much trust Grandpa Adolph either, not since that day a few years after his marriage to Hannah when he took her engagement ring in to be reset and learned from the jeweler in the Mount Royal Hotel that his father-in-law had sold him a flawed diamond. Nor did Lazar trust, or much care for, any other member of Hannah's family. *Litvaks!* was the ostensible explanation, even though he knew that the name applied to Lithuanians, not Latvians. (*Kurlander,* as Latvians called themselves, was not the strong expletive that Lazar needed to describe his in-laws.) His distrust also had to do with some unspecified sums of money not paid back by someone whose name was never spoken because at just this moment Hannah always hissed *Der kinder!* so sharply that even Lazar would shut up. (We read the *Katzenjammer Kids*; we knew what that meant.)

Adolph was such a religious man—holy, even!—that during the war years he made his living by teaching Hebrew. On Yom Kippur in the Spanish and Portuguese Temple, where the women sat upstairs behind a screen, he joined the men in front of the Ark and stood next to the one who had all the fun of blowing the shofar. Adolph had grown up, Grandma Freda never tired of telling all of her grandchildren, in Hasenpoth, a town whose name was pronounced in a tone that made it seem to be a vast, imposing place filled with great scholars, musicians, and rabbis—a grand city like Paris or London. Grandpa certainly did not come from some muddy village that swarmed with mosquitoes and Gypsies. Which was to say that Adolph was most definitely not from Romania but from a civilized country, one where people (and this was the only stab at wit that any of Freda's descendants ever heard her attempt, as well as her only known public reference to Lazar's profession) *did not make books but read them.* She would never say such a thing when Lazar was around, for everyone knew that, like all Rumanians, he had a *terrible temper.*

It is difficult to know what Freda found more galling—having to call on Lazar's mother, Sarah (her senior by two decades), that ignorant old woman who spoke only Yiddish and who bathed only once a month to judge from the smell around that apartment. Or having to eat that garlic-laden Romanian food that Hannah had been taught to cook by her sisters-in-law: stuffed cabbage, cornmeal mush that they called *mamaliga,* chopped liver and eggplant (both with so much oil), and those heavy meat pies that they insisted on calling *progen* even though everyone else called them piroshki. Or having to live with the realization that her Adolph, the Hebrew teacher, was for many years the most successful numbers runner employed by Lazar and his brother, Moishe.

Of the hundreds of men they employed in the late thirties, none was better on the streets than Adolph. Even French-speaking workers seemed to feel that buying a weekly ticket from a man in rabbinical garb was bound to bring luck, and the fact that Adolph had once dreamed of becoming a rabbi made him convincing in the role. How could his customers know that just for their benefit Adolph— in one of his rare moments of business acumen—had purchased a new black suit when he went to work for Lazar and Moishe? Nobody in the family had ever seen him dressed that way, and the first time he appeared at the Rotenstein house wearing the outfit, my brother David fled from his own grandfather, thinking him someone sent from the Sha'ar Hashomayim to tell his mother he had skipped Tuesday afternoon Hebrew class.

Adolph had to buy the new suit because, for all his rabbinical air, he had been a jeweler since the age of fifteen and his wardrobe consisted entirely of dark gray, double-breasted suits. Dark gray seemed to suit him. Years later his grandson, Rabin, would imagine that it was as if the Latvian landscape of his early years, the endless bogs and lowering skies and stony beaches and chill waters of the Baltic, had somehow entered Adolph's soul. When his grandchildren were tiny, he would bounce them on his knee while chanting a children's rhyme in German: *Hup, Hup, pferding,* but his voice was never playful. He smiled rarely, and then with a strange, alien expression that seemed pasted on the surface of his face, an expression that could serve equally as a response to a pun made by his son-in-law or to the sight of a grandchild with a knee scraped bloody on the stones of a playground after a fall from a swing.

Adolph could display a certain kind of humor when things became painful. Like the pain of realizing that his grandchildren were straying so far from the faith that they were no longer (in his eyes) Jews. This became most apparent during the brief period when Rabin's older brother, Chaim Baer, lived with his grandparents after the rest of the family had moved to California. Chaim Baer did not put on *twillin* and pray in the morning. He did not go to temple on Fridays. He ran around with Zionists, who were, as everyone knew, completely godless. On the morning of Yom Kippur, after Adolph had hurried off to the temple, Freda found his reading glasses and gave them to Chaim Baer to take to his grandfather. Late to a screening of Eisenstein's recent film, *Ivan the Terrible*, Chaim Baer didn't even bother to enter the temple, but merely handed the glasses over to someone at the door. That night at dinner Adolph looked directly at Chaim Baer while he spoke to Freda: *Who in heaven's name did you get to deliver them? The shammes told me they were dropped off by some goy.*

Once a year, on Passover, Adolph took charge of things. Over the objections and complaints of everyone in the family, he insisted on reading each and every word of the Haggadah, a process that seemed to last forever. On these occasions her husband's religiosity did not make Freda happy. The service was repeatedly punctuated with her stage whispers: *Hurry, Adolph, hurry up, for God's sake. Skip ahead. My roast! Der kinder!* But mere words could not move him. Adolph droned on through the plagues visited upon the Egyptians as if by chanting slowly he could make the miseries of these enemies of the Jews last forever. Perhaps it was just as well. By the time the ceremony was finally over, the grandchildren were hungry enough to eat anything—even Freda's roast.

Despite his vast learning, Adolph was a man of simple tastes. He might speak English, German, Hebrew, Yiddish, Russian, and Latvian, but when it came to food he liked nothing better than boiled fish and potatoes. With a little *zenf.* Adolph liked *zenf.* That, in fact, was about the only taste that Adolph had in common with son-in-law, Lazar. They both liked *zenf.* And, of course, they both liked Hannah, Adolph's eldest daughter and Lazar's wife. Not that you could be certain of this. Neither was demonstrative. Lazar yelled a lot, especially at Hannah and at his eldest son, Chaim Baer. Adolph never raised his voice. When he was upset, he gave a good hearty chuckle, put on his hat, and left the house.

The only vice that Adolph seemed to have (if vice it was) was an immense fondness for *the movies.* Cousin Morty, who played hooky from school, claimed to have seen Adolph's bald head in the front row of the Gayety Theater during one of Lily St. Cyr's annual engagements, but none of us dared believe him. Once, twice, sometimes three times a week, Adolph would put down his German or English newspaper, rise from his armchair, don a hat, and announce to any and all present—his wife, Freda; their perpetual boarder, Mr. Rosenthal (who did not seem to have a first name); any of the children or, later, their spouses or the grandchildren—that he was off to a movie. Since Montreal law forbade anyone under sixteen from attending a theater, we were especially interested in movies. The next time we saw Grandpa, we would pester him with questions, but talking to Adolph about a movie was—though we could hardly know it then—like dealing with a great oracle or Zen master:

What did you see?
A movie.
What was it about?
Goyim. Movies are about goyim.
Who was in it?
Who should be in a movie? Actors!
Did you like it?
What's not to like?
What did you like about it?
It was a movie!

When Freda Voss was eight years old, a dairymaid who was her second cousin was one day seen riding through Hasenpoth in the splendid carriage of Baron Von Raden, sitting next to the baron, who smiled and leaned over her attentively. Nobody knew how or when the two had met, or if or how long they had been lovers, but the point soon became moot when the young couple eloped to Germany, never to return to Latvia. Were the girl's parents pleased or angry to receive a letter from Berlin saying the two young people were now married? It's difficult to say. The baron was not, of course, Jewish, but he certainly was rich. Skeptics were sure that such a mismatch could not last for long, but years later one of Freda's younger brothers would visit the baron and his wife in their grand home atop a hill on the Isle of Capri, and he found them happy, generous, and gracious hosts. The ex-milkmaid who was now a baroness asked to be remembered to everyone in the family, and especially to her cousin Freda.

This event was Freda's only known contact with nobility of any kind, but it seems to have made a powerful impression on the young girl. No doubt it fueled those broad hints she liked to drop for her grandchildren about *royal blood* in the family, though out of some sense of personal modesty she always attributed this honor to Adolph's line rather than her own. The claim that her husband was a bastard offspring of the czar of Russia, secretly given to Adolph's family to raise, was surely a way of getting back at Adolph's mother, a woman who had attempted to stop the marriage on the grounds that Freda was not high class enough for her son. Such a tale was also a kind of retroactive escape from the poverty and misfortune that marked her early years. Freda's mother had died when the girl was eight, the oldest of five children, and it fell to her to raise the younger kids. Her father was poor, ineffectual, and incapable of keeping a job. Her grandmother, who lived with them, remarried four times to get out of the house—but every one of her husbands died soon after the ceremony and she had to move back in with Freda and family once again.

Nobility was something you could hold on to. Nobility had land, castles, servants, traditions, money. Half a century after serfdom had been abolished, peasants in Hasenpoth still kneeled in the streets when the baron rode by in his carriage. And a half century after that, in the apartment on St. Mark's Place, always filled with the gloom of winter afternoons no matter what the season, beneath the imitation Dutch still lifes depicting cows, fields, dark groves of trees, and chilly looking rivers, amidst the heavy, wooden furniture, the worn velvet sofa and chairs with antimacassars, the age of royalty lived on. You could find it behind the locked glass doors of Freda's own bookshelf, where thick leather-bound memoirs of life at the courts of Europe crowded against each other. The presence of such books underwrote a social life that consisted of afternoon high teas served on bone china, teas taken with gray-haired women who would never let a word of Yiddish (heaven forbid!) pass their lips but who liked to flavor their conversation with a few words of *hoch deutsch,* teas that always ended with Freda at the door, saying to each departing guest, *Danke schoen fur besuch.* It was a phrase that both her daughters would repeat after their own dinner parties all of their lives.

To begin with, naturally, would be about myself.

At the age of eighty, Adolph would publish his first (and only) book, a memoir entitled *The Way It Was* that covered the first thirty-two years of his life. The work was printed by a vanity press in New York and paid for by Adolph's eldest child, Elliot. To tell the truth, Adolph did not exactly write the book, but dictated the words in a shaky voice to one of his granddaughters on her Sunday visits to the hospital. Not that Adolph was illiterate. At one time or another he had been able to read and write German, Russian, Latvian, Hebrew, Yiddish, and English. But the strokes and heart attacks that made Room 219 of the Jewish Hospital of Hope his final residence also made it difficult, but not quite impossible, for him to hold a pen firmly enough to form words on a page. In the copy of this book that came down to his grandson Rabin, Adolph's signature is there in large, shaky letters on the flyleaf.

Adolph Kramer. Author of one book. One life.

To begin with, naturally, would be about myself.

When his grandson first read that opening sentence in the mid-sixties it made him cringe. So did the following paragraphs and pages of this weepy immigrant narrative, a classic tale of rags to (comparative) riches that was burdened with homilies, bad grammar, historical inaccuracies, and a passive acceptance of injustice— personal and social—bound to annoy any young contemporary with pretensions to social activism. Leave it to an aspiring writer in his mid-twenties like Rabin to overlook the possibility of originality.

To begin with, naturally, would be about myself.

Perhaps the sentence was a mistranscription. Certainly Adolph's speech was more than a little slurred when Rabin visited him in

Room 219 in 1958 on his way home from Paris, where he had just spent several months desperately trying to imitate the behavior and prose of the literary figures he had been taught to admire—Hem, Scott, and Dos. Now *they* were men who knew how to write sentences. Crisp sentences full of the vigorous, if disillusioned, attitudes of privileged middle-class Midwestern men discovering that Paris is not Des Moines. Poetic sentences full of echoes of Shakespeare and the King James version. Ironic sentences with nuanced insight into the self-destructive actions of various drunks and artists.

To begin with, naturally, would be about myself.

Perhaps it was a matter of mixed grammars—of the uncertain way in which his many languages fit together. But as he read the work over a period of two and three decades, Rabin had come to a better appreciation of his grandfather's life and the prose in which he rendered his adventures. He came to see that opening sentence as a highly self-conscious literary device, a move meant to throw down the gauntlet to Melville:

Call me Adolph.

The statement is unusual in its honesty. No matter how much an author may protest in the name of higher powers and larger purposes, one naturally must always begin with oneself, and just as naturally in the conditional—that is, in a state of doubt. Like anyone indulging in autobiography, Adolph (in his late seventies and early eighties) had to wonder: Did these things really happen to me? Are the memories, the ideas, the experiences really mine? And these words I write, or dictate—to whom do they belong?

The story his grandfather told, Rabin would think after his college courses in the British novel, could have been scripted by Dickens: His birth in 1880 in the Latvian village of Grobin, population 1,000, which boasted two synagogues but only one rabbi. The tragic death from pneumonia two years later of his father, a substantial storekeeper, a death due to the fact that his very ill parent could receive no medical treatment because the only doctor in the tiny town had—could this be true or was it some odd impulse toward slapstick?—committed suicide on the very day the pneumonia reached its *critical stage.* The attractive mother in her mid-twenties who married a grain merchant with children of his own and sent Adolph off at the age of nine to live with a great aunt in the substantial town of Hasenpoth, a mother who then departed with her husband for Rotterdam without even bothering to say goodbye to her son. The death of his aunt and the beginning of a nightmare. For two years Adolph suffers the humiliation of becoming a football, kicked around for meals and a nightly bed from the home of one indifferent, distant relative to another. Worse follows: he is pulled from high school—he loves his studies of German and Russian, history, geography, math, and science—and apprenticed to a jeweler, a certain, classically cruel Herr Aronsohn, who will work him without respite twelve hours a day, six days a week for the next five years. These long hours do not prevent a desperate attempt at self-education that has Adolph reading works in German and Hebrew by dim candlelight into the early hours of the morning, or hiking long distances twice a week to attend classes at the high school, or even longer distances (there is, apparently, no such thing as a short distance in Latvia) to borrow books from his single friend— Freda Voss, niece of the high school teacher and a distant relative who at the age of twelve has been raising four younger children while serving as an apprentice to a dressmaker.

Adolph and Freda are fifteen when they kiss for the first time, an emotional meeting of lips on the eve of his flight from Latvia without a passport. He goes by coach to Libau, where a friendly innkeeper hides him in a hollowed-out bed to avoid a police check. He joins a group of pitiful refugees *fleeing to freedom* across the German frontier at night, led by a guide who at the last minute demands extra *blood money* to keep from rousing the border guards. A train takes him to Memel, then Berlin, and on to Holland, where he finds that his mother is not, as her letters had claimed, poor and downtrodden, but in fact the manager of her own business, a woman who dresses in silk, lives in luxury, and displays little interest in caring for a teenage son. The contrast between her world and the *dinginess and poverty* of the life he has been living in Latvia is so great that within him springs up a feeling of *bitter resentment* that will last for the rest of his life. Adolph cannot understand why she has ignored him and why she has lied to him. Sixty years later in the Jewish Hospital of Hope, her behavior will remain a painful mystery.

He moves again, this time across the Channel to London where he struggles to get established as a journeyman jeweler, learn a new language, and keep from breaking the Sabbath rules. For three or four years he puts in his time learning his trade, traveling to the midlands and to the north, working for generous bosses and cruel ones, finally saving enough to send Freda a ticket to come from Hasenpoth to England. Their courtship lasts for three years—Adolph works in shops, she in factories, and the distances between where they work and live are so great that rarely do they get to see each other except on those occasional Sunday afternoons when they stroll through a park or visit a museum. But the great day arrives at last. Theirs is one of seventy-five marriages performed at Stepney Green Synagogue on a rainy August 17, 1902, two days after the coronation of King Edward VII in Westminster Abbey—an event that will allow Adolph to say *I was not invited because I was busy getting married myself.*

The next nine years see the birth of four children—Elliot, Hannah, Schloime, and Lena—and a continuing search for a better place to work and live. In 1906 Adolph sends Freda and the kids back to Hasenpoth while he goes off to the New World. It seems, at first, a great mistake. The revolution that has broken out in Russia swirls into Kurland and threatens the family. In Montreal Adolph opens a store that soon fails, and he must forsake his trade for manual labor. On a bleak, frosty morning he begins to work in a rubber factory, where he must lug enormously heavy bundles of material, twelve hours a day, for $3.50 a week. But winter passes and spring always comes—in seasons, in life, in memoirs. The family manages to get out of Latvia and make it to Montreal. Adolph opens a second jewelry store, which also fails. Undaunted, he goes back to work for someone else and then soon tries a store once again. This time, wonder of wonders: it prospers. Soon he is owner of a second store, and then a third, for which he pays an enormous rent of $10,000 a year. It is 1912. Adolph is thirty-two. It is a moment he will remember until his deathbed.

I had come a long way from Hasenpoth and a longer way from Grobin and I was grateful to the Good Lord for his many blessings. I had a loving wife and four beautiful children. I was putting down roots in a new community—in a new world. With Freda by my side, I could now face the future with more confidence than I had ever known before.

For years his grandson Rabin imagined that the break in the narrative just when Adolph opened his third store at the age of thirty-two was due to illness, to the fact he was too weak to carry on any longer. But like the opening line, it makes more sense as a conscious artistic move, the construction of the story of an immigrant by an immigrant who has learned his immigrant stories well. As a devotee of movies, Adolph had to know the proper time to conclude a narrative was while standing on a symbolic pinnacle, at a moment of expectation when you can gaze off toward a bright future. Life, we all learn, will take care of itself—the dashed hopes for economic success; the future that darkens year by year; the bright and beautiful children who grow up to be not so bright, not so beautiful, not so successful, and not so honest as you had hoped; the feelings of love and companionship that cannot remain the same as they were in Hasenpoth, London, or Montreal in the early days. In any tale for future generations, it is important to know exactly when and how to say good-bye.

Adolph—or was it his son, Elliot?—chose not to end the book in words, but with a dark and faded photograph. Wearing a black suit, Adolph stands facing the camera, his face shadowed, his expression blank and unreadable as he looks directly at us, Elliot on one side of him and Schloime on the other, the slightest of suppressed smiles beginning on their lips, while in front of them are the two girls in white, seated and unsmiling, Lena with a bow in her hair, Hannah with a hint of the wanton in her shadowed eleven-year-old eyes. The caption is terse—*A Sunday afternoon in Montreal 1917*—but Rabin finds it strangely evocative. Almost as strange and evocative as the fact that Grandma Freda is absent from the photograph.

Even when they were very young, Adolph's grandchildren found it odd that such a learned, religious man went so often to the movies and lectured them so little—less than did Grandma Freda—about the glories of Hasenpoth. On rare occasions Adolph would quote great rabbis and Talmudic scholars, or refer to obscure events in the history of Latvia or Great Britain or the Jewish people. He had a bookshelf of thick volumes with dark, close-set print and no pictures. But rarely did anyone see Adolph read anything at home other than the newspaper. In the early evening he would sit for hours in his huge armchair, staring at the long list of numbers that are the stock market reports, occasionally muttering *Aach* to himself.

He might closely follow the market, but Adolph had no head for business. True, a certain energy that brought Adolph from Hasenpoth to Montreal also brought him those few years of business success, and the three jewelry stores he owned led for a short time to visions of a chain of such stores stretching across Quebec, Canada, the entire continent. But this was one immigrant success story that was not to happen. Adolph might understand watches, but human beings baffled him. The manager of his second store, his half brother, vanished one day between lunch and closing time with all the watches and pieces of jewelry that customers had left for repair, along with the store's stock of stones, costume jewelry, finger bands, brooches, earrings, pocket watches, chains and fobs, wristbands, blank keys, eyeglass frames, jeweler's tools (including three magnifying eyepieces), and all the cash—no more than thirty dollars—that had accumulated since his midday visit to the bank. A couple of years later, the third store proved unable to meet the challenge of a shop on the next block owned by a newly arrived jeweler from the Ukraine who, along with nine children, lived on the premises and worked for almost no profit.

The first shop continued to support the family, but by the mid-1920s Adolph had his eyes on wider horizons. Tinkering endlessly at his workbench, Adolph had somehow connected a clock mechanism to an alarm and come up with one of those ideas clearly worth a million: a burglar alarm for automobiles. This was the decade of the auto, a time when an American president won office on the notion of a chicken in every pot and two cars in every garage. Surely every one of those car owners would feel safer if his car had an alarm that went off if someone attempted to steal it. There were, of course, some technical problems to be worked out. For half a decade he labored to perfect the mechanism. All the family savings went into building prototypes, purchasing two demonstration cars, and sending Adolph off to New York City to market the product. He had been there for two years when finally an executive at Chrysler decided that yes, it would be a good idea to put the alarm on every one of his company's automobiles. But the very day before the meeting to iron out the final details (or so the story goes), this far-sighted man dropped dead of a heart attack. His successors would have nothing to do with the alarm, and so Adolph returned home, a broken man who never shared his deep hurt with anyone.

Whatever the problems involved in working for his son-in-law (and that flawed ring never ceased to rankle Lazar), the numbers were good to Adolph. It was not just the money, but the liberation from the problems of owning stores, from the constant upset with employees, customers, suppliers, and banks. It was also a liberation from indoor life. On the streets he was free to stop in a restaurant for a cup of coffee or a bar for a schnapps, or (perhaps) to slip into a movie or a burlesque house for an afternoon show. Adolph's conscience no doubt prevented him from wholeheartedly approving of the way he was now forced to make his living, but he was enough of a believer to know that such choices are forced upon one by higher powers.

These same higher powers reside in Adolph's book. More than a simple story, the work is a reflection, a meditation on memory, loss, hope, and desire, the search of a modern self to find a place where it could fit into a shifting world of landscapes that in retrospect had to seem stranger than when he initially encountered them. Think of the changes he experienced. The move from muddy, one-street Grobin to Hasenpoth with its fine stores, large Apothecary, and splendid Adliger Club for members of the nobility. His first visit as a teenager to relatives in the city of Libau with its broad, paved streets and boulevards *like a dream,* its banks, hotels, jewelry stores with *imposing and luxurious fronts,* its six-story buildings and electric streetcars with plush interiors, its grand parks, and magnificent beach, and harbor where foreign ships lay at anchor. Later comes London, that seat of the greatest of empires, a monster with its endless web of streets; with Parliament building, squares, monuments, and bridges; with free spaces like Hyde Park, where speakers were *sounding off and expressing their opinions on everything under the sun from politics and religion to health fads and personalities.*

You can say that Adolph felt blessed by God and history. The two were connected. As a child in Grobin he might enjoy the romance of playing with friends in the ruins of castles built half a millennium before by Livonian Knights, but the history that mattered was the one that set him free. In Kurland relatives disappeared into the czar's armies for twenty-five years to fight against the Turks, or were prevented from teaching without a government certificate that was impossible to obtain, or from traveling from one city to another, or from freely choosing their own trade. Holland was different; the Dutch had welcomed the Jews since the fifteenth century; the country and his people had prospered together. The same was true in England after Cromwell had invited them to return. The British were a fair people, an outspoken people. Here even as a poor foreigner, even as a Jew you could hold your head up and speak your mind and be treated decently and never have to bow your head. It was a place where he felt at home but for one thing: opportunity. Only in the colonies could you make a dream of wealth come true. But wealth, or happiness, or that indefinable feeling, that something that sets a man on the road from Hasenpoth may never be capable of satisfaction:

We always hope for something which never materializes—it was almost always that way with me.

· ·· ‗ ‗ ‗‗‗

Only after his death at the age of eighty-six did it become apparent why Adolph had, many years before, so much trouble answering questions about movies. On those nights when he put on his hat and left the house to see a film, he was in fact going to see his mistress. Evidence for this part of Adolph's life accumulated gradually. A granddaughter found some odd items at the bottom of his dresser drawers after they moved him to the Jewish Hospital of Hope: lingerie, girly magazines, and letters of recent date full of erotic descriptions that were addressed to half a dozen women. Following that, it was a matter of inference (especially by his grandson Rabin), supplemented by an adroit question posed here and there to parents, aunts, and uncles whose minds were, in their seventies and eighties, a lot more vague than they used to be. Now they occasionally forgot the hushed tones, the fingers to the lips, the unwillingness to admit a single negative fact about one's parents or grandparents that was so extreme you might think the family to be devoted disciples of Confucian ethics.

About the mistress, we don't know much. Except that the relationship lasted almost as long as Adolph's marriage. Let us say they first met during that brief period when Adolph, then thirty-two, owned three stores, including a large, fancy one on St. Catherine near Bleury for which he paid such a high rent—$10,000 a year— that he would rightfully boast in his autobiography: *I had come a long way from my little apprentice bench in Herr Aronsohn's establishment in Hasenpoth.*

Picture it as late morning in this store. His assistant, no doubt with magnifying glass stuck in his eye, is at work in the back of the store repairing a pocket watch. The store owner, having dusted the counter, the clocks, the glass shelves, and finished by wiping a few specks off the ornate mirror, is taking time to admire his own reflection, the image of a square-faced, solid man in a dark gray suit who has a slightly enigmatic but definitely self-satisfied smile pasted on his face. The bell over the door announces the arrival of a customer, but before he can put on the proper face for business, another image appears in the mirror—rouged, high cheekbones, messy strands of blond hair escaping from under an elaborate hat, leather-gloved hands clutching a fur (fake, but how can we expect Adolph to see that?) close to her body. Was she there to buy a new timepiece for herself, one of those brooch models that were becoming so popular, and did he help to pin it on her dress? Or was it a gold-plated watch, a present to assuage the guilt that regularly swept over her for the husband she had never much loved and now thoroughly despised? Or was it to have the clasp on an earring fixed, and when she hands it to him does Adolph admire the sweet lobe of the naked ear on which it belongs? Certainly she had to return to pick up the item within a few days, and it's a good bet that on this occasion they for the first time left the premises together—just, mind you, for a cup of Earl Gray tea and a few petits fours and only, you understand, to discuss how to provide for long-term financing for the marvelous gold necklace that Adolph had, *I can hardly believe it, you crafted it yourself,* and which would set off her hair and her complexion—*well, it's as if you had me in mind when creating it.*

The second meeting, the third—the gestures, the conversation, the double entendres (if any), the life stories (full of sorrow and misunderstanding): the details all lead to a hushed moment one afternoon or (less likely) evening when for the first time they face each other alone in a hotel room rented to Mr. and Mrs. Allan Kay of Toronto, on a bed where they find that their bodies understand a language neither of them has ever before spoken. After that, it becomes a matter of careful arrangements, discreet intervals, late nights at the store taking inventory, business meetings, and movies, which, as Freda says, are *so cheap they give me a headache. So go, Adolph, you go on alone. I'm happy to stay at home and listen to Elliot play the piano and read a good book.*

Does Freda find out? How can she not? For a long time she suspects that something is going on but doesn't really want to know. Then a friend lingers after the others leave a tea one afternoon and says, *Well, you know, someone, not me, saw your Adolph with this coarse blond in the elevator at the Windsor Hotel, I can't imagine what he sees in her, and they were…* Soon Freda makes it her business to learn more: the woman's name, Magda; her nationality, Hungarian; her address and phone number; her husband's name and profession. When this sorry man dies prematurely, four years after the affair has begun, Freda uses the phone number and demands a meeting with Magda.

Does Adolph learn about this meeting? Of course not. No more than he ever learns that his wife and mistress will remain in contact until Freda's death more than thirty years later. The meeting, a congenial two-hour encounter, centers around a deal proposed by Freda: *You don't try to take him for your own and I will never make any objections about you.* Magda agrees: yes, it would be best to share him. Who knows, after all, which woman a man would choose if he were pushed to a decision and what would be the point? Each, for her own good reasons, is happy to have no more than half of this man. Adolph has his good points—he is educated, clean, responsible, and for Magda at least, a passionate and yet respectful lover. But let's face it: he doesn't speak much, his sense of humor is heavy, and neither Judaism nor the stock market are subjects women wish to discuss at length. So the bargain between them sticks for all those years, and even though Freda and Magda never see each other again, they talk with regularity on the telephone. When Adolph is sick, or depressed, or in trouble over business, they confer. When Magda needs a temporary loan, Freda sends a check. When Freda worries over the inability of her old-maid daughter Lena to find a husband, Magda provides introductions of eligible bachelors. When Adolph is away in New York, they commiserate, though each one suspects, wrongly, the other of going down to spend time with him, and each worries that in Manhattan he is involved with yet another woman.

He isn't. At least not until after both Freda and Magda die within six months of each other. His second wife, who survives for only six years with Adolph, looks and sounds exactly like Freda. What the grandchildren are never able to figure out was whether the lingerie in his dresser belonged to Freda or to his second wife or even to somebody else. Names on mailboxes revealed that some of the letters in his drawer were addressed to women who lived in the same building. Were they, his grandson Rabin would wonder, no more than fantasy missives? Or were the letters in the drawer because the women had died before Adolph was able to deliver them? Or had he slipped the letters into the mailboxes or even into the pockets of his neighbors as they stood in the cold foyer of the apartment building, buttoning coats and talking of the awful weather, and had they returned the letters to him, flattered but fearful that their husbands or children would some day find these erotic notes? In any work about the past, one can create a number of different stories from the same traces of evidence. Rabin, who did go to films several times a week, came to believe that the story of Adolph's life would make a damn interesting movie.

To begin with, naturally, would be about myself.

My father, the dandy, in an undated photo probably from the twenties, his and the century's, about the time he was working out a lot at the YMHA and taking on all comers in the ring. The spiffy, if traditional, suit must have been handmade, as were all his clothes (including his shoes) as long as he lived in Montreal.

THREE

Lazarus West

H. R. 79557
6th Congress
3D *Session*

In the House of Representatives
January 16, 1940

Mr. Bates of Massachusetts introduced the following bill; which was referred to the Committee on Immigration and Naturalization

A Bill
For the Relief of Lazar Rotenstein

Be it enacted by the Senate and House of Representatives of the United States of America in Congress assembled, that notwithstanding the provisions of the Immigration laws, Lazar Rotenstein, whose wife and family are permanent residents of the United States, shall be granted a visa and admitted into the United States.

N o matter how vague his mind, no matter how foggy his memory, no matter how often he mistook his sons for his long-dead brothers, his wife for his mother, his grandchildren for playmates in the long-forgotten streets of Tetscani, Lazar Rotenstein never became reconciled to Beverly West. As such places go (*It should have gone,* Lazar would have added in the old days), it was not too bad—clean enough, with edible (more or less) food and attentive nursing. Yet for four—or was it five?—years he never stopped hating it. Who could blame him? Never when you came to visit was he in the TV room, or the dining room, or the lounge, or the sun room, or his own room, which he shared with a succession of men whose names he never cared to know. To visit Lazar, you had to search along the endless hall of the square building built around a central courtyard, a hall which he ceaselessly patrolled in his wheelchair, occasionally bumping against patients who were not agile or alert enough to get out of the way. At the end of each visit, when you were about to leave, Lazar would say, *Let me come home with you.* Later it was impossible for Rabin to recall when his father had begun to add, *Just for tonight.*

With regularity, Lazar escaped from Beverly West, upsetting the staff and leading to demands from the dark-suited director that he be made to behave *or else.* The threats had no affect upon Rabin, who was proud of his father's escapes. They seemed to recall his years in the rackets, though Lazar had never been jailed and only once detained by authorities, and that for a single day when he was caught attempting to cross the border into Cleveland with a trunk full of betting cards. During Lazar's longest absence from Beverly West, his son David, the lawyer, stood in the lobby for most of an afternoon, talking in a loud voice to a succession of worried administrators about the lawsuit for negligence that he was ready to file, one so large it might well close the doors of the institution. Lazar was found snoozing in the doorway of one of the cheap nearby hotels for veterans on Sawtelle shortly after David went home with a sore throat. When Rabin asked Lazar what he had done for the last twenty-four hours, the old man replied with a wink.

Staying at Beverly West for more than a few minutes was an impossible ordeal for Rabin. He hastened his father away from the smells of disinfectant and urine, the moaning people tied to chairs, heads slumped on their chests, or standing blank and stunned in the hallways, as if struck blind from staring at the sun too long or turned to stone for looking back on the forbidden cities of their own past lives. He buckled Lazar into the seat beside him and drove swiftly past the country club on San Vicente and the joggers in shorts to the bluff above Santa Monica Bay, where the palms—much taller now—had fired Lazar's heart during winter sunsets half a century before, on that fateful trip to his (supposedly) dying sister's bedside, the trip that changed his family's life. His financial decline, his brother Moishe's rise—all because of a startling postcard moment of beauty beneath those trees.

Such thoughts belong to his son. Lazar's mind is focused wholly on Beverly West. His conversation consists entirely of complaints about the food, the smells, the inmates, the staff.

Take me home. It's not healthy to live with these sick people!

Dad, you're sick too.

Sick, schmick. A big gesundheit! They're old!

Listen, you're no spring chicken.

But they're really old!

· ·· —— — ———

After the first strokes, when he was still living at home with Hannah, Lazar had enjoyed telling elaborate stories about amorous adventures during his time as a door-to-door salesman in the provincial towns of Quebec in the late teens. Conversation with young ladies was difficult, and much was lost between their meager English and his meager French with a few words of Yiddish thrown in when all else failed. But Lazar was resourceful, willing to try anything that might work, that would help to move a female toward his shabby hotel room, or into a field where frogs sing to the rising moon, or into a graveyard beneath the crosses of those who now sing in heaven, or onto the couch in a living room crowded with overstuffed furniture, or into a dim pantry where the rocking motion of two erect bodies makes the shelves of jars full of berry preserves clink and rattle precipitously.

Love has consequences. Back in Montreal, Lazar receives a letter from a small-town girl whose face he cannot remember: *We have a beautiful baby boy. He looks just like you. Why don't you come to visit us?* He never does, but fifty years later he wonders aloud to his son, *Maybe I should have.* Rabin, stunned to think that somewhere in rural Quebec a man he will never know shares half of his genes—has his nose or eyes or receding hairline—and perhaps half his desires and dreams, says, *Yes, weren't you curious? You should have gone.* To which Lazar gestures impatiently with his right hand and says, *Ah, g'waan!*

The most improbable of all Lazar's stories had a French farmer lead him to a bedroom where his daughter lay waiting with legs spread wide. When Lazar finished with her, the farmer's wife entered the room for her turn, and when that was over, the farmer came in to present Lazar a round and juicy rear end.

Dad, you didn't.

Lazar nodded.

C'mon, Dad. You've got to be kidding.

Lazar looked hurt.

Would I kid you?

You do all the time.

Not this time.

His ass? His ASS? C'mon, Dad.

You never had to sell anything. You think it was so easy?

Once he got to Beverly West, Lazar would no longer talk about his early adventures or about much of anything else. Politics, the economy, the usual depredations of *the big interests,* the resurgence of fascism, Jews and/or Canadians in the entertainment industry, developments in Israel—in none of these did he any longer take an interest. Nor did he care to talk about other members of the family— Rabin's brothers, Chaim Baer and David (who visited as regularly as Rabin), their wives, Hannah's relatives, Cousin Sheila or Aunt Ida, Morty who now lived in Tel Aviv, Hymie who was carrying on his father's bookmaking business in Montreal. Strangest of all, he no longer mentioned his big brother Moishe and all the money he still owed Lazar.

One day Lazar announced, *I'm an orphan,* and a tear rolled down his sunken cheek with its patches of gray and white stubble that the attendant never got quite smoothly shaved. It was true. They were all gone. Moishe; Mendel, the baby, who had gone to sea and come home with an Australian wife one week after Rabin was born, a woman teased at every family gathering for the next sixty years for her heavily accented remark over the crib, *Oh look at the buy-bee;* Tilly, whose *homentaschen* were the best in the world; Polly and Franny, with their beautiful legs and eyes made vivid by makeup; and Rosie, the only one to marry a man who refused to join the rackets, the only one who had to vacation at Workman's Circle, with its communal kitchen. At the age of eighty—or eighty-four—Lazar was truly an orphan, or an immigrant once again, stranded in an alien land with a visa that would soon expire.

· · — ══

If your eyesight is very good, if your mind is suitably concentrated, if the angle of the afternoon sun on the serrated surface of the Pacific is just right, if the clouds are gone and the breeze calm and the beach almost empty and only a few white sails scud slowly across your retina, then it is possible to stand on the bluff in Santa Monica beneath the palms and watch the snow fall in Montreal. It is always snowing in Montreal. Drifts pile deep against the flat brick facades of duplexes off of the Main. Iron stairways are icy and your ungloved hand sticks painfully to a curving banister. An arctic wind blows through the city—starting north of Hudson's Bay, it skims the Laurentians, roars past Back River and over the homes of gentiles in Westmount, blasts down Sherbrooke to Bleury, swirls in a permanent storm around a small, chilled figure standing on a street corner.

Lazar Rotenstein is selling newspapers—what else?—and not after school. (*As if he goes to school!*) His day of labor begins early. Seven times a week he rises from his makeshift resting place on a humpbacked trunk (*See how lucky you are to have a bed, a room of your own?*), eats a ball of cold *mamaliga,* and trudges off through snowdrifts, weighed down beneath a sack that remains impossibly full and heavy no matter of how many copies of the *Gazette* he tosses onto front porches. The exact hour of his departure and the precise number of miles covered each day are both a matter of some historical debate. Did Lazar, as he sometimes claimed, rise at four to walk five miles? Or was it five to walk four? Or three to walk six? And what, you may ask, ever happened to summer in the first decade of the century? (Yes, these are the voices of his sons—his discrepancies of memory are their delight. How could they not be? The boys are heir to a peevish sort of humor that, like flat feet, will pass from one generation to the next.)

Lazar on the street corner, then, a figure in sepia tone or out of an

Lazarus West 47

early sound film, a Bowery Boy or Dead End Kid in a long bedraggled coat, overly large cap set at a jaunty angle, and scuffed boots, standing amidst snowbanks that grow taller each passing year, crying *Extra! Extra! Read all about it!* But newspapers are not his only connection to the written word. Like everyone in the family, he has little formal education. When six weeks of public school in Tetscani made him the most learned Rotenstein, his parents pulled him out of the classroom and set him to work in his father's shop. In Montreal, he never attended night school, or worked with a tutor, or joined a labor union education group, or attended classes at Workman's Circle, and yet somehow he learned to read English. Asked how, he answered: *I taught myself.* Not that Lazar ever read with ease. His lips formed the words as his eyes moved slowly across the page, a man edging through a dangerous, unfamiliar landscape. Yet every afternoon in the early forties, Lazar read the Mother West Wind story in the *Star* out loud to Rabin, and in his twenties, he evidently had managed to get through as much of the writings of Karl Marx (not very much) as ever did his son, *the writer.*

My son, the what?

Did any other immigrant father ever possess such a vision? Imagine: somewhere Lazar reads *a article* (all his life he will begin paraphrases of published pieces with the phrase *I just read a article*) explaining that at the moment of conception all (*ALL!*) a man has to do is to concentrate on whatever he wishes his offspring to become. So when he arrives for a weekend to visit his family, who are spending the summer of 1935 in—what a poor joke, Rabin would think—Schroon Lake, arrives at the white Victorian hotel with the broad veranda and broad green lawn, and when he comes to Hannah in the white room where the white curtains blow in the twilight breeze off the lake, Lazar is far from his own sweating body and his wife's body, far from the smell of genitals, the starch of fresh cotton sheets, the squeal of springs, the flutter of moths against moonlit screens. Far into some dream of words to voice the longings of his heart.

· · --‗‗‗ ‗‗‗‗

Only in his stories of traveling rural Quebec, or sporting in the bedroom (if sport he does), is Lazar alone. In every other story of Montreal in the twenties he is always part of a team. Lazar and Moishe. Moishe and Lazar. (Names can be prophetic: one seemed to be a leader of men, the other to have walked among the dead.) On the Main everyone knew them—the butchers, greengrocers, bakers, barbers, and candy-store owners; the yeshiva *bucher* and the rabbis in stained coats, collecting money; the touts and pool hall sharks; the men who sold shiny metal toys from suitcases open on the sidewalks; the hookers with bruised eyes. Two well-dressed young men with a quick stride, the round-faced one (leader of men) smiling, the long-faced one (back from the dead) trying not to stare too directly at you with those startling, oversize blue irises. *Nu, nu!* they call into stores—*Nu, Nu!* to friends across the street. *Wie gehts? Wie gehts? Wie gehts!* Not stopping, no time for that. Hurrying always toward some great and important deal.

Inseparable. Moishe and Lazar. Lazar and Moishe. Always called The Boys by family and friends. Worked together and played together; ate together at Ben's deli, went together to the YMHA (Young Men's Hebrew Association) on Park Avenue for a fast game of handball, a *shvitz* in the steam room and a rubdown; bought cokes together for teenage French girls in the garish dance halls east of Bleury on Saturday nights; made the same jokes about these girls in the same mock French accent; owned a Model T together and took Mother out together every Sunday for a ride in the country. Never did she look more regal than when she sat erect in the backseat, broad-brimmed black hat and black coat powdering with dust. Never did they realize that her expression, that fixed smile on her face, had nothing to do with pleasure, that she had been terrified of cars ever since seeing the first one in Tetscani three decades before, that she went only to please the boys: Kaina hora, *they're so proud of their car so how could I get them upset?*

For Mother the best time of the week is Friday night—the candles, the *chalah,* the prayers (though none of the family ever goes to temple), the presence of (almost) all the children: Rosie but usually not her husband, who is off somewhere probably talking against the shul and the rabbis. Polly, sometimes with her American husband, a mensch who treats her right, dresses her in silk and furs, so who cares if the trip back to the States is in a truck full of bottles the Americans with their goyish laws don't want. Tilly and her man, Charley, who talks too much, jokes too much, drinks too much schnapps—but upholstery, that's a good profession, never get rich but always have a job. And Franny, beautiful Franny, with a *schoene* man even if he is a Litvak, *but he can teach my Moishe and my Lazar a thing or two about those horses they think I don't know anything about. As if their office fools me. But Mendel, the baby, he's gone and up to no good, I know it in my bones. Just like his father, that one; he'll be off, he'll be back; he'll never have a dollar in his pocket; he'll marry God knows when, God knows what. But the other boys, God keep them from marrying as long as possible. Kaina hora, it's a sin but it's so happy to still have them at home.*

· ·· ⎯⎯⎯⎯

The first of many offices that Moishe and Lazar rented was in the corner of a large suite occupied by Princess Jewelry Ltd., manufacturers of fine costume jewelry. That the space had to be let showed that the old Montreal firm was falling on hard times, but this did not mean lowering all standards. When the brothers arrive in response to an advertisement, the office manager looks them over carefully, notes their neatly manicured hands and immaculate summer shoes, and decides that, despite heavy accents and large noses, they will make good tenants. No doubt he is a touch mystified that they decline his offer to have their names, or the name of a company, painted on the frosted glass that separates them from the main secretarial room, but he is certainly too polite to question this decision.

Rarely do the brothers arrive at the office before midafternoon. As they troop through the suite, the company secretaries—quiet girls who have managed to make it through the business course at Montreal High—sigh audibly, except for Hannah Kramer, who keeps sighs and everything else to herself. Every day, the same routine—a wink here, a nod there, and then the glass door gently closes. From behind the partition, the hum of male voices is low at first, but soon the sounds grow louder and the voices rise, and then rise again, and then again until even if you are not listening (and Hannah surely was not, for her mind was on Julius, who would meet her under a streetlamp to recite poetry, his own poetry, in a breathy voice that smelled of garlic), you can hear the anger. Still once again the voices rise, and now the two men are shrieking in the high-pitched cries of some beaky, ill-tempered jungle fowl. For fifteen minutes. Thirty minutes. Up to an hour. Then at last the voices grow soft, the door opens, and nodding right and left, Moishe and Lazar leave the office as softly and politely as they arrived.

Here's the problem: You could make over the outside, but the inside stayed the same. You could dress well, even conservatively, but for people used to talking Romanian or Yiddish, it was difficult to be soft. You could conclude deals, but didn't know how to read contracts in English very well. You could hire lawyers, but their lawyers knew the judges. So it was best to do business with your own. A handshake, a clap on the shoulder, a quick schnapps, and besides my sister's married to your cousin Schloime. Best of all, you should hire relatives, however distant they might be. Or at least Romanians, they're crazy but in ways you understand. But whoever you hire and whatever business you do, nobody comes to the office. Money changes hands in the front parlor while Mother is in the kitchen baking *progen,* or honey cake, or *homentaschen,* as only Romanians make them, stuffed full of honey and walnuts. The office contains no typewriter, no stationery, no envelopes, no telephone. Only a few scratch pads for notes written with the expensive fountain pens that they carry in their inside coat pockets.

—————

Some time in the mid-1920s Lazar bought a Stutz Bearcat, a sweet, cream-colored machine shiny with nickel plating. Moishe never forgave him, just as he never forgave him any of the cars after that— the front-wheel-drive Cord; the luxurious Pierce-Arrow; the black Packard with its wide whitewalls and pinstriped upholstery; the postwar Studebaker with the wrapped windshields that made everyone joke about not being able to tell the back from the front; the succession of Cadillac Coups DeVille, each longer, chromier, and harder to handle than the one before. The final Caddy, a two-tone green '57 with enormous tail fins and a gold V below the hood ornament, was so large that Lazar could barely see over the dashboard, and his normally erratic driving edged toward the lethal. His children sighed with relief when, after the second stroke, he was forbidden to drive. For years the car sat in the garage of the apartment on Holt Avenue, and every time Rabin visited, he would dutifully run the engine for ten minutes to keep the battery charged, *just in case.* Then one day in the early eighties it was gone. Lazar rubbed his hands as if he had made a killing and explained he had sold it to a handyman for five hundred dollars. His son could not bring himself to explain it was worth ten times that much.

The impulse stirred by the Stutz found other outlets. Strolling along Sherbrooke to an appointment one spring day, Lazar stopped and stood for a long time before a painting in the window of an auction house, a still life in which every detail was so startlingly real— not just the petals, pistils, and stamens of the irises and lilies and other flowers he couldn't name bunched in the glass vase on the table, but the caterpillar crawling up one stem, the red ants on the lacy tablecloth, the flies with diamond-shimmering eyes hovering in the air, the beads of water about to drip off the leaves, which if you reached out and touched the canvas would, he was certain, feel wet. A few days later, he attended the auction, purchased the picture for a considerable sum, brought it home, and gave it to his mother, who seemed dubious about accepting it.

Who needs a picture, she asked. *Did it cost?*

Naah, it didn't cost. It's a nice picture. Hang it over the mantle.

You're sure it didn't cost?

I like it, Mama. It looks so real. Don't you like it?

What's to like? It's a picture.

It'll look real good above the mantle.

Okay, you like it I'll hang it. But only one. Don't get another. It'll cost. One picture's enough.

Moishe, who didn't see the point of the picture either, always drove a Buick. No matter how wealthy he became in the 1950s, no matter how many buildings he constructed for great international corporations, no matter how many donor-of-the-year awards he won from United Jewish Appeal of Canada, no matter how many scholarships or classroom auditoriums at Technion Institute in Haifa bore his name, no matter how much his daughter and wife might plead for a Lincoln Continental or a Mercedes-Benz or a Jaguar, Moishe ordered a new, gray Buick sedan every two years until they only came in colors like Sand, Sunset, Iceberg Pink, and Jetstream Blue. Then he let Sheila choose the color.

Moishe always favored solid gray suits, with white shirts, and dark neckties, while Lazar dressed in patterned woolens, in herringbones and tweeds, in fawns, soft blues, and chocolate tones with shirts that were creamy, or tinged with pink or heliotrope, and ties splashed with flowers or bright patterns. All his clothing was made to order and each piece had his initials stitched onto a cuff or lapel, or under the silken label of an inner pocket. For morning workouts at the track, Lazar—who was never actually seen mounted on a horse—was handsomely clad in a hacking jacket, jodhpurs, and handmade English riding boots.

But wait. What is this Roumanian immigrant doing at a racetrack in the morning? Watching the stable hands put his horses through their paces. Moishe had objected to the investment—*Bet on the damn things, but why buy them? You're so in love with horseshit?*—the first business venture they did not go in on together. In truth, Moishe enjoyed the weekend afternoons at Blue Bonnet's, leaning over the rail and cheering on his favorites, and there was a particular pleasure he took in always betting against Lazar's horses. This proved to be a mistake. Two of them, Wilkes-Barre and Ambulance, won a number of stakes races and earned a good deal of money for Lazar, money he was able to bank because unlike Moishe and everyone else in the family, he never really liked to gamble—and certainly he would never risk money on something as chancy as a horse race.

By the mid-twenties, no doubt about it, Lazar had begun to suffer from the sins of vanity and even pride (if sins they are). He certainly was proud of his large wardrobe. Proud, too, of the increasingly muscled body underneath all the fine clothes. Physical culture was becoming the closest thing he had to a religion. As business grew more and more profitable, he spent more and more time at the club, lifting weights, playing handball, getting massages, preening in front of the mirror. Some obscure desire moved him toward more violent sports. Wrestling was good; boxing was even better, the blood and exhaustion of even a short match proved a nice release for those feelings that so often erupted into anger against those close to him. More and more did he boast about his agility in the boxing ring, especially after winning some decisions in club tournaments and scoring a knockout that surprised Lazar as much as his opponent, a haberdasher he normally faced across a counter full of neckties.

Sport did not make Moishe happy, but Lazar's final appearance in the ring provided him with some brotherly joy. Nobody remembers the year, but it was the one when the brothers acquired a carnival and led a caravan of trucks across the border and south to states where for the first time they became familiar with black faces and heard white men speak of Jew bankers ruining the niggers, the country, the world. Of all the concessions in the carnival, the brothers kept one for themselves: *Step right up, gentlemen. Easy money. Stay in the ring for three short rounds with Tiger McHorn and win twenty-five dollars!* When they returned to Montreal and put up tents and a midway on the expanse of Fletcher's Field, McHorn, whose real name was Rosenblatt, decided there was more future in his father-in-law's delicatessen than in the ring. Nobody seemed to know where the brothers found his replacement, or what was this bruiser's nationality. When he received fifty dollars at the end of each week, the man grunted and signed the receipt with a wavering X.

The new McHorn was so huge and ferocious and unbeatable that crowds began to dwindle. What to do? In the name of profits, with only (perhaps) a dash of vanity, Lazar—after Moishe said that he would tell McHorn to take it easy—climbed jauntily into the ring and danced up and down, enjoying the shouts, the catcalls, the whistles, and you'll-be-sorrys. His confident, crooked smile lasted nine seconds into the first round. McHorn's first right made it apparent that either the brute did not understand English or Yiddish or French, or that maybe he understood the theory of surplus value and knew damn well who was paying for that Stutz and those monogrammed shirts. Lazar took enormous blows, dropped to the canvas, hung on the ropes, hurled himself desperately into clinches, tasting the salt of his own blood and whispering fiercely, *Carry me, you fucker, carry me.* Give him credit: he lasted two minutes and fifty-three seconds into the round. The doctor set his nose in the dressing room, while he was still unconscious, but it was bent slightly to the left for the rest of his life. The dental work took three office visits.

Later they owned businesses that were far more successful than the carnival. They shared suites of large offices, hired secretaries, purchased letterhead stationery, and dictated memos and letters. Freehold Finance, General Metal, Millen Freres Lumber, M&L Cord Agency, Beaumaire Plaster—each was a legitimate enterprise; each was also a front for the real moneymaker, something they called *Policy* and other people would call *Numbers.* Much to the surprise of everyone (including himself), Lazar sometime during the thirties invented a payoff system based on the sum total of the weekly football scores that proved easier for customers to understand than the previous one based upon the stock market index. Moishe specialized in setting up franchises, dealing with government officials, and handling relations with others in similar rackets. The business expanded until almost everyone in the family—cousins, uncles, aunts, spouses, nephews, nieces—was working for The Boys. By the late thirties, they had subsidiaries in seven cities from St. John's, New Brunswick, to Kingston, Ontario, and were talking with people in Cleveland about crossing the border. During these waning years of the Great Depression, when five dollars could buy you a four-course meal complete with French wine in the dining room of the Ritz Carlton, Moishe and Lazar were bringing home a thousand a week—and paying no taxes. A few years later, during the war, the weekly take of each went up to five thousand.

In January 1937, when their sister Polly lay on her deathbed in Los Angeles, Moishe delegated Lazar the family emissary to say a farewell. He was happy to go. Unlike Moishe, who always seemed to take Polly's marriage to an American as a personal affront, Lazar understood his sister's desire to get away from Montreal. When he left Windsor Station there were six feet of snow on the ground;

when he returned one month later, eight feet. For three weeks in California Lazar strolled on summerlike beaches, picked oranges from trees, stared at the palms that grew into black cutouts against sunsets that seemed tropical. Polly—false alarm!—out of bed by the second week of his stay, drove him down cheery streets lined with startling pink, peach, and yellow bungalows and into dusty canyons that smelled of sage. Everyone on the platform—Hannah and her sons, Adolph and Freda, Ida and Moishe—was astonished by Lazar's first words when he stepped off the Pullman car of Delaware and Hudson's Manhattan Limited: *We're moving to California.*

Lazar was interested in politics. As a teenager he was committed enough to some Young Socialist group to mount a soapbox on a corner of the Main and speak about the need for an international brotherhood of workers. More than once he had to flee when cops or goons from some nationalist party waded in to break up the rally. His profession might change, but he never lost his youthful sympathies for The Workers. In the thirties, to keep up with what was going on in the world, he read both the *Star* and the *Gazette.* He knew about the threat to democratic Czechoslovakia posed by the Sudeten Deutsch; he cheered (and surreptitiously gave money to) the Loyalists in Spain; he worried about the possibility of German *Anschluss* with Austria; he was certain that madman Hitler was going to start a war. What he had failed to learn about was American immigration law. In the six months after his return from California, he sold his magnificent home on Upper Belmont (purchased but two years before from, he would ever after report, a French count who could not pay his bills and was, therefore, *No 'count*), liquidated his business holdings, worked out a rather unfavorable ongoing silent partnership arrangement in the numbers with a furious Moishe, and sent almost all of his period furniture and antiques, acquired over the years at estate sales—the Sèvres, the Capa di Monte, the Wedgwood, the Rosenthal china—off to auction houses where they were knocked down for a fraction of their value. When someone mentioned the need for an American visa, Lazar was surprised. Filling out the forms at the consulate took five minutes. A clerk informed him that processing would take longer.

How much longer?

Mr. Rotenstein, you were born in Romania. The quota for Romanian immigrants is one hundred a year. Your kids are native-born and your wife is from England—they can all emigrate now. You can plan on joining them in 1960 or so!

For the next decade the Rotenstein family moved about like Gypsies, twice residing in hotels (the Mount Royal and the La Salle), the rest of the time living in rented places, a duplex on Sunnyside, a house on Vendome, the double apartment on Maplewood. Lazar acquired a new supply of antiques, including an early nineteenth-century, inlaid French baby grand piano, two sets of English bone china, a good number of still lifes in oil, and one smallish copy of a hefty Cabanel Venus attended by flying *putti* that had won the grand prize at the Paris salon in 1873. He could afford such luxuries because the war years were even better for him than the Depression had been. Full employment, overtime work, and fat paychecks meant there was lots of money for gambling. Lots of money, too, to circumvent American immigration law. Lazar never revealed how much it took to have an attorney in Hartford and a Massachusetts member of the House of Representatives get a *special relief* rider bill passed by the U.S. Congress in 1940. Its aim: to allow poor Lazar Rotenstein to join his wife and children who were already (in theory) living in the United States.

The years lie between them, wordless. The wordless years always lie between them. The light is fading, the palm trees turning into silhouettes.

Mendel, it's a nice day. Let's drive to Ottawa.

That's a long way off.

I know. But it's a nice day. We can stay overnight.

You have to be back by five.

Mama will worry. I know. We can stop and phone.

Listen, Dad. We're in California, remember?

I know a nice hotel in Ottawa.

Dad, Ottawa is too far to drive and I'm not your brother Mendel. I'm your son. I've got to get you back to the hospital.

Mendel, did I ever tell you about Tiger McHorn?

Sure.

Moishe did it.

What, Dad?

Fixed me good.

What do you mean?

Fixed me good. In the pause Lazar made a sound, but Rabin could not tell if it was a sob or a snort. He did not look happy, but then he never did.

I fixed him too.

Another pause, while a hundred cars roar by on the highway below. Two hundred.

Mendel, Moishe hasn't written to me in a long time.

He's dead, Dad, remember? He's been dead for four years.

Yeah, I know.

Listen, we've got to go. I've got to get you back to the hospital.

Moishe's rich. The least he could do is phone.

Wild Hannah as a teenager. The eyes and expression say it all.

FOUR

Wild Hannah

Tuesday, Nov. 20th, 1923 Rather a banner day for me seeing it is the first time I played a really big number as a solo. It was a bridge at the Spanish & Portugese, and Mrs. Rutenberg introduced me ever so prettily. Naturally, I played my famous, (or otherwise) Fantasie Impromptu by Chopin. I was extremely nervous until I got to the piano, and then I shed it like a cloak. The runs just RIPPLED from my eager fingers, and I played the whole number with a fire and energy that startled even myself, accustomed as I am to my peculiar moods. But I was ever so determined to make a success, and I verily think I did. There were about a hundred and fifty people present. They clapped loudly, DEMANDING an encore. I gave them, unwillingly, I must admit, my dreamy, lovely, vague Lotus Land. In direct contrast to the vivid brilliance and showy technique of the other number, it therefore shone brighter in view of this difference. The sweet and plaintive notes of a lovely melody trickles through the piece like honey. It took instantly. I heard several people gasp with astonishment when I played the entirely unexpected "glissando." There was a moment's hush when I had finished. And then the applause was tremendous. Excitedly I ran around like a wild little colt let loose. My cheeks were aflame with the scarlet colour that came and went. And my eyes sparkled with selfish wonder. Everyone congratulated me. Gee, I felt great. My vanity was highly gratified, and I was satisfied.

Wednesday, Dec. 18/23 What a queer chord those Russian books strike in my heart! First Anna Karenin, and now, The Spy by Maxim Gorky. How morbid, how unusual, especially, the latter. This book is degrading to my morals, but still, fascinates with the attractions of "Forbidden Fruit." I am horror-stricken by the freedom of thought and living,

I am disgusted with the vulgarism of the uneducated, and still I read, more,…yet more.…In my mind there is the subconscious thought that all this tends to broaden. But I am stricken again with a feeling that has accosted me often of late, is it all in the name of Vanity only? What else gives me that satisfied glow of work accomplished well. Whenever I hear something I invariably, exclaim mentally, "another point to the good" and promptly feel happy again experiencing that pleasurable glow. The heights are beautiful joyous and incomparable, but the depths are inevitable. The transition occurs without warning, instantaneously, and now a feeling of despair grips me in its throes. Can this thing be VANITY? And my unhappy heart answers "yea."

I told Olga I couldn't come for my lesson. Even my music seems very unsatisfactory to me today. A lazy inclination has settled o'er my head, and my brain is wrapped in drowzy fumes which tend to suffocate any attempts at self-analysis. I wish I were simple and stupid, and not always anxious to learn things which only serve to heighten my inane curiosity, and strengthen the desire to gaze into unsounded depths.

FROM THE DIARY OF HANNAH KREISLER

The streetcar took Hannah past Fletcher's Field twice each day. She watched the tents going up, the midway being pieced together like a giant, colorful toy. She saw the empty grounds glistening in the morning rain, and the after-work crowds beneath colorful banners buying tickets at red-and-white kiosks and pushing through metal turnstiles, and the posters for the world-famous boxer, Tiger McHorn. When the workload was heavy at Princess Jewelry and she had to stay late, she could see strings of lights swaying softly against the night and heard, in those moments when the racket of metal wheels ceased, the sounds of tinny music, far-off shouts, and shrieks of joy, fear, and wonderment. Every day it was as if she lived for a few passing minutes amidst the sweaty crowds—stuffing on hot dogs, drinking sarsaparilla, marveling at the tattooed lady and the midgets, watching someone (some handsome man) hit fifteen consecutive bull's-eyes and then turn and present her his trophy, a huge doll with spun gold hair and china blue eyes. No wonder she felt a sense of loss that morning when the Ferris wheel was gone and the boards of the fence down, leaving only a frame of posts, while huge pieces of canvas, spread on the trampled grass, were carefully folded into giant sails by crews of boys. No wonder there were secret tears over the vast, empty twilight park where pigeons strutted beneath the trees, mothers pushed prams, boys in short pants sailed boats in silent stone basins.

Even if she could have afforded the entry fee (she gave Mama her entire seven-dollar salary each week save for the fifty cents for tram fare), Hannah would not have been allowed to enter the carnival grounds. Such places were unsafe for young ladies. Nobody of breeding should even want to go there. At least nobody from a family in which all the children took piano lessons, even if it meant that a boarder named Mr. Rosenthal filled the third bedroom with his bulk and his cigar smoke and the top shelf of the icebox with his food. Nobody from a family with all those books, bound in leather, behind the glass of the cabinet in the parlor. It was always locked because Mama let you know that *some people were still too young to read everything,* particularly de Maupassant and Balzac, even if they were classics.

Twelve-year-old Schloime knew how to get the cabinet open. Once he offered to share a forbidden book with Hannah, but when she took it in hand her heart beat furiously and her eyes couldn't focus on the words. It was much like the feeling that time on the streetcar late one night when in the corner of her eye a well-dressed, middle-aged man raised his newspaper and she saw his unbuttoned pants and could not stop staring as his hand pulled out something disgusting. Her eyes snapped shut and she sat rigid for a very long time until her stop was called, then she rose and fumbled toward the door and only when she was safely on the traffic island after the folding doors hissed shut did she glance back and see that he was no longer in the streetcar.

You could not go to a carnival for the same reason that on those rare occasions when you did get to the Laurentians for a few days you could not go swimming with everyone else even if you were almost seventeen and had been a breadwinner for almost a year.

Mama and Papa did not know how to swim, and they had heard too many stories of children eaten by whales, carried away by undertows, swept by treacherous currents out to sea.

But Mama, Schloime would argue. *It's a lake. There's no whales. No currents. It doesn't connect to the sea!*

Send them to school and they know it all, replied Freda, gesturing with empty hands toward the sky. It didn't matter for Schloime. He snuck off to swim with friends anyway. But Hannah was too frightened to follow, and besides she had to care for baby Lena, didn't she? On the one occasion when she was allowed to go with Sadie Richler's family to their house in St. Agathe for the weekend, she could have tried the water, but her fear was too deep, so she claimed it was that time of the month and sat on the dock and watched Sadie and her brothers and their dog swim to the raft, splash about, and call back to her. After two days, Hannah could hardly wait to return to Montreal.

In the city she had an active social life. With girlfriends she went to movies and to tea rooms, where they sat up very straight in their chairs, took dainty bites out of tiny cakes, and did their best to look like real ladies. Their adult posture was betrayed by the endless giggling and all the talk about a single topic: boys—who was the cutest, the smartest, the richest, the best dresser, the best prospect for marriage. Knowing her ideas on the subject to be unusual, Hannah did not contribute much to these conversations. She could appreciate looks, clothing, and money, but other notions touched her as well: something about the mind, the heart, the soul, something about creativity, about books, music, Kultur (which she always thought and spelled in the German manner); something about friendship and exploration—wasn't life a kind of adventure, shouldn't all these things be part of marriage too?

The only one who could understand such notions was older brother Elliot, who sometimes read to her paragraphs from Nietzsche and Schopenhauer and secretly lent her volumes by Russian novelists. Brother and sister both took lessons from the same piano teacher, but he was the more gifted. Hannah practiced diligently and regularly. Elliot noodled around on the keyboard whenever the mood struck him, yet in his midteens he began to compose songs and then got a job playing in a movie theater. When Freda objected to both the *low-class* venue and the late hours, Elliot moved into a boarding-house, worked longer hours at the theater, and began to spend his free time with a woman who suffered, in his family's eyes, from two unforgivable defects: she was several years older than he, and she was not Jewish. He still came to dinner once a week, but it was never again quite the same between brother and sister. Even when they managed a walk around the block together, all he wanted to talk about was New York. That was the only place where a songwriter could make a career. He was putting away all his money. Soon he would be on his way to a bigger world.

In contrast to her brother's shining future, the situation at home seemed hopeless. Adolph's jewelry store was not doing too well, and working to keep the family going on so little was making Freda prematurely old. Everyone's hope rested on Schloime—he would go to medical school and become a success, but that was a number of years away. Sometimes Hannah fancied that the piano could be her way to fame and fortune; she would become a great concert artist, tour the world, and return to Montreal to play at the Princess Theater. But no matter how much sadness, desire, hope, and expectation went into the endless hours of playing scales and practicing Chopin études, the teacher always qualified her judgments with a criticism that Hannah never knew how to meet—*technically that was fine, but it needs more feeling; you need to make us feel the music more deeply.* The pinnacle of her career as a soloist came on a Tuesday night when, as a bridge between two lectures at the Spanish and Portuguese Temple, she performed the *Fantasie Impromptu* to an audience of one hundred fifty people who clapped so long and loud that she returned to the instrument and played an encore, *Lotus Land.*

Her seventeenth birthday meant a wider social life. Hannah was still too young to date, but it was OK for mixed assortments of boys and girls to go bowling, or to motor into the country for a picnic (some of the most popular young men had automobiles), or to attend dances at the Maccabean Circle or the Young Men's Hebrew Association. Plain of face and never quite able to master the rhythms of anything other than the simplest fox-trot, Hannah was popular enough for her high spirits, obvious intelligence, rosy cheeks, curvaceous figure, and shapely legs that went so well with the skirts that each year climbed closer to the knee. With regularity, young men from nice families professed their admiration, even their love for her. The boldest, in dark corners or hallways or in the backseats of cars, expressed a wish for a *goodnight kiss*. Some pleaded, some argued, some threatened to do it without permission, but no matter how much a young man's desire excited her, Hannah always said an absolute and definitive *No*. When she really liked someone, Hannah could question her own resistance to temptation. But sex was so *holy and beautiful* that to pollute its sacred quality with *mere vulgar passion* seemed *absolute and utter treason*. Yet she did not want the boys to stop asking. Teasing gave her great pleasure; remaining cool and unaffected by a man's passion produced a strange sense of joy.

The first man to kiss Hannah had onion and garlic on his breath. Her nose and eyes watered as they pressed their mouths together, but she didn't pull away, not even when she felt the sweet, scary sensation of his hand gently on her breast. Julius could not help the smell—she understood that. He lived on a diet of potatoes, onions, and garlic, for his salary from the medical laboratory and the money he earned from tutoring went directly into the bank, where it would remain untouched until he entered medical school. Julius wore a bedraggled coat and his collars were frayed, but on the long walk to meet Hannah in the evening, he composed poems that he whispered into her ear in the stale hallway of the apartment building or under the fluttering glow of a summer streetlamp on Dorchester. She never asked him why the lines did not rhyme because what mattered more was that his words, spoken so passionately, seemed to be full of her own secret aches.

On the streetcar to work, Hannah sometimes wrote answering poems in her mind, but never did she commit them to paper or voice them aloud. When they were together, she asked lots of questions about books and philosophers and even biology, and she loved his slow, patient answers. He had read everything and knew everything and was happy to share what he knew. Best of all, he was not going into medicine just for the money but in order to do serious research, to find a cure for polio or tuberculosis or other diseases. Sometimes he helped Schloime with his science homework, and after he left the apartment Mama called him *a nice boy.* But going off to medical school in Paris?—*well, there's lots of French girls, don't you know, Jewish French girls too.*

No promises were every promised. In their many months together, only once did they ever speak of *marriage and its divine possibilities.* It was the week before his boat was to sail for Europe, and the words all belonged to Julius, explaining slowly, patiently, with infinite tact and understanding *how absolutely impossible it would be in our case.* Their last meeting was on a park bench on an October evening as balmy as midsummer. Julius recited a farewell poem he had just written, then he recited it again. Fifty years later some of its phrases would still haunt her. *As each weary day drags on. . . . I long I crave, for the repose of the grave.* What would always remain to Hannah of Julius, what she would pass on to Rabin, the only one of her sons who would listen to such things, was a vision of a bowed figure in long muddy coat dragging through rain, hail, sleet, and snow, a figure tramping for miles with wet feet in order to save the nickel for a streetcar, a mind brimming with poetry and chemical formulas, a bad complexion from too many potatoes, breath potent with garlic and onions, the early winter evening (for it is always winter in Montreal) gathering around him like a troubadour, a daydream, a hero out of old storybooks, or novels no one any longer reads; and then Julius shrinks, dwindles to a small point of brightness, becomes a feeble candle that suddenly winks out.

· ·· ═ ═ ═══

Listen to Freda on marriage:

Some people you don't marry. Poor boys you don't marry. Polacks you don't marry. Romanians you don't marry. Hungarians, maybe, it depends. Take my own sister, Rachel. Off alone in St. John's, New Brunswick, with the two babies, while Izzy's gallivanting around God knows where. She's the beauty of the family—such white skin, such silky hair, and he's such a beast, so homely with one eye higher than the other and those eyebrows, it's disgusting. She didn't have to tell me about the wedding night; it was over long before that. But if that's what you want, I told her, that's what you get. It's your life, so don't come crying to me. Only you'd think he'd support her at least and not run around with all those crazy ideas that were bad enough in Russia. You can get into plenty of trouble here too. Imagine Rachel having to work as a nurse and the two little ones, kaina hora, *not getting to school half the time. But no, Izzy's a big shot. My sons aren't going to be bar mitzvah, he says, just like that. And Rachel goes along with it as if she believed all those things too. He's so smart he still has to come to Adolph for money and then all you get for an answer is that laugh and Don't worry, soon nobody will have money, there won't be any money. That will suit Mr. Big Shot just fine because he never has any money anyway. It makes my skin crawl when he looks at Rachel so disgusting, and once when she was in the kitchen fixing tea he looked at me that way and I almost screamed. If I ever catch him looking at Hannah that way, I'll kill him. She's just a girl and she's got to get married soon. Not a holy man like Adolph—someone who's fine only on Shabbas. She needs somebody with a little push, but not too crude. At least he should know what a book is and have a job and not want to turn the world upside down just because it doesn't suit his lazy ways.*

· · ── ── ──

Later Hannah could not remember all the details, nor the exact sequence of events. Lazar Rotenstein smelled fine, of soap and some subtle cologne with a touch of man-smell coming through. The furthest thing in the world from onions, and when there was garlic on his breath (for he was a Romanian after all), it was covered by the bitter, pleasant odor of *sen sen,* which he always carried in his pocket. He looked fine too, always well dressed, his thinning, light brown hair well trimmed, his nails manicured as nicely as a woman's, his eyes big, startlingly blue, and sincere. Close up, his voice was not nearly as loud as all those shouting matches behind the glass partition would have indicated, though in truth it was not too soft either, and there was an accent, but not too heavy. So when he stopped by her desk that December day, when he sat on the edge of it to chat about the weather or whatever, she was so surprised that without thinking she said yes of course she could go out with him on Friday evening, even though in the past she always had asked Mama for permission beforehand.

He picked her up in his car and first took her to see Lon Chaney's *Hunchback of Notre Dame,* which Hannah found *gruesome and horrid.* Then they bundled up in a hired sleigh for a ride to Mount Royal and laughed so much she *nearly croaked.* Finally it was off to dinner and dancing at the Edinburgh, the fanciest place she had ever been. Hannah did her best not to react too much to the steep prices on the menu, but this part of the evening was miserable because his brother's girlfriend, Ida, was so loud and so drunk, and Hannah's dress, made by Mama, who—*Never forget it, young lady*—had supported herself and her family as a dressmaker in Hasenpoth, *where people knew how to dress properly,* was so dowdy and out of place, and she couldn't even follow Lazar decently on the dance floor. It was such a surprise that when, letting her off at twelve-thirty, he said *How about New Year's Eve?* that again she said *yes.*

A lot of tears got Mama to agree just this once to a store-bought dress, because after all you are going to be eighteen soon. The Doronna was even fancier and the prices on the menu exorbitant—*five dollars a plate.* She tasted champagne for the first time, and it made her feet move well on the crowded dance floor, and after three or four glasses Ida seemed like a pretty good sort after all. Amidst the hullabaloo of midnight, the dimmed lights and candles and streamers and funny hats and shrieks and words of *Auld Lang Syne,* he kissed her softly on the neck and then he popped the question. She was too startled, too bewildered to answer, so back at the table he repeated it in front of the others, who were all blowing noisemakers and raising glasses of champagne and grinning and shouting across the now-stained linen, and what she heard herself saying, softly so the others would not hear, was *I'll give you an answer if you ask me when you're sober.* Two days later he arrived just after supper hour carrying a two-pound box of the finest chocolates and a dozen red roses. Without knowing what yes would mean, what after all could a girl say?

Two people objected: Mama and Moishe.

A Romanian? Big talkers. They're all big talkers, but you never know what's true with them.

A Litvak? Well, Albert's OK for Franny, but he's a special Litvak. At least he knows how to get a job done.

High livers. You never know where their money is going.

The old man's going broke. He doesn't like to work. All he cares about is the Torah and movies.

Doesn't surprise me that the mother doesn't speak English after twenty years. Did you see a single book in the house?

So she plays the piano. Who ever heard of a Litvak who could cook mamaliga. Or anything else.

Mrs. Knadlach has a brother-in-law who has a friend whose sister used to know a girl whose boyfriend worked for the two of them. Don't you know what business they're in? It may have to do with books, but it has nothing to do with literature.

Fifteen months later, after two postponements, the wedding took place at the Ritz Carlton, which means that contrary to tradition, Lazar must have paid the cost, for how could Hannah's family have afforded this most expensive of Montreal hotels, and how could he have gotten married anywhere else and still looked himself in the mirror and his friends in the eye? The postponements were painful. First Moishe, demanding his right as the elder, insisted that his own wedding took priority. Then Lazar had to plead an unspecified *business reversal*. Somebody had welshed on a debt—no doubt a member of the family, maybe even Moishe. Mama shook her head knowingly, then after Lazar's departure, she sent Hannah into tears by insisting, *He's trying to get out of it.* Mama was, in truth, pleased with this development—she did not like Romanians, but that objection alone had not overridden the desires of her for once willful daughter.

Even Adolph emerged from his normal, blustery silence to say: *He's got a good income. He looks nice.*

But he's ten years older than Hannah. And he's a Romanian.
Aaaach, said Adolph, in a tone of disapproval. Then he put on his hat and went out to the movies.

The wedding dinner was so beautiful, and Lazar and his two brothers so handsome in the glossy black formal dress suits with tails, and his sisters so much like gorgeous blossoms with their fine legs showing beneath shining silk dresses, and the bone china and sterling silver and Irish linen and cut crystal so dazzling that Mama was almost ready to forgive them for being Romanians. In her own wedding dress the bride was lovely, but Hannah felt overshadowed, somehow withdrawn in the presence of all these voluble, excitable, dazzling women who were now her sisters-in-law. Maybe it was the edginess from her period, two weeks early and more painful than any previous one she could remember. Or the lingering doubts, the feeling that perhaps Mama was right. Such thoughts would not do at all, and she reached again for the champagne glass. It was her second evening of champagne, her second evening of whirling around the dance floor with Lazar, who led her smoothly from waltz to fox-trot to waltz again, round and round to his brothers and Papa and Boris and little Morty, so cute in a formal velvet suit with knickers, and to Mr. Rosenthal and even Izzy, who stumbled and smelled odd and smiled more oddly, and then back to Lazar's arms and to his cousins whose names she always forgot and then to Lazar and Moishe and Lazar and always with a champagne glass whirling in her hand with the ballroom lights reflecting diamond arrows off the chandelier, whirling in dance until elation became tears at the corners of her eyes, and whirling was dizziness and Hannah was waking up in a strange room with the second upset stomach and a mile-wide headache and a man looking both familiar and strange in pale blue silk pajamas was gazing down at her with some expression midway between a smile and a frown. She had never seen a man in pajamas before, because Papa always wore a nightshirt, and when she asked desperately for a glass of water, the man in pajamas—her husband?—held out his right hand like a traffic policeman and shook his head and said *No. Water will only get you drunk all over again.* True or not, this answer made Hannah uneasy. Who would like having her first request as a married woman denied?

They went first to Niagara Falls, then to New York City, but later neither of them would be able to remember exactly where the marriage was consummated. Five decades later Hannah would say this: *He was like an animal. A brute.* The conversation was unique and the tears in her eyes highly unusual. Lazar was in the hospital again, probably dying after yet another stroke, and Rabin and his mother sat in the apartment, drinking tea from some of the fine bone china cups that she had begun to collect shortly after the wedding trip when Lazar gave her a cup he had pinched from the Ritz Carlton. Rabin and his mother were eating the delicious butter cookies that she had learned to bake from his sister Tilly over half a century before, only these days they were either tough or tasteless because she always seemed to forget at least one ingredient, and Hannah was saying things that Rabin really did not, at this or any other moment, wish to hear: *I know he bragged a lot, but he didn't know anything about it. And I never learned anything because he never taught me.*

They lived in a one-bedroom apartment with a maid, a young French girl, who slept on the couch in the living room. Hannah had little to do but practice the piano and learn how to cook. (*Romanians like spicy food* was the single bit of premarital advice she had received from her mother.) Lazar would not touch the boiled white fish, boiled potatoes, and boiled carrots that were Adolph's favorites, and when she could find no Romanian cookbook at Eaton's, she had to turn to his sisters for recipes and advice. It was humiliating, but soon she could cut up garlic cloves and onions without crying, cook brisket until it swam in dark brown gravy, bake the *progen* with just the right flaky dough, chop the liver by hand and mix it with tons of schmaltz, prepare the slimy eggplant and olive oil that she did not taste herself for more than twenty years, and cook up pots full of the bright yellow *mamaliga* that sent Romanians into moans of ecstasy. Soon enough Hannah found that Mama's food, when they went over for the weekly dinner, was too bland for her own taste, even though she would try to swallow as much as she could when Mama said, *Eat child. You're getting thin as a bird.*

It was not true. How could she get thin when she had nothing to do. Social life was mostly with Lazar's family, or other Romanians who seemed to be almost family, and no matter what the location, there was always too much food. The family still made Hannah feel stiff, reserved. Sometimes she tried to talk about books or music, as she always had with Elliot at home, but nobody in this family played an instrument, and though all the men pored over the daily newspaper, nobody was ever seen with a book. Only after a while did Hannah learn that except for some Hebrew study prior to bar mitzvah, Lazar was the only one of the seven brothers and sisters to have ever gone to school. After six weeks in a village school when he was seven years old, Lazar was pulled out of the classroom. What was the point of continuing? He was already the most educated member of the family.

When the gatherings were at their apartment, Hannah liked to show off the linen closet, with the ironed sheets, pillowcases, tablecloths, and napkins neatly folded, arranged in ranks, and elegantly set off by a slender piece of satin that started under each pile, rose across the front, and then lay over the top. Each was embroidered and placed so that you could read the lettering that designated the items below— *pillowcases, sheets,* or *guest towels.* Hannah was proud of this display, especially so because none of her sisters-in-law could match it. Every time the clan gathered at their place, Lazar insisted she perform. Hannah always played Chopin's *Fantasie Impromptu* on such occasions, and while she proudly ripped through the work, everyone was politely silent. A chorus of applause and *bravos* would crash over the final notes, then everyone would return to shouting and joking. Hannah was always disappointed that nobody asked for an encore.

Rabin found Hannah's diary among some papers when they were breaking up the estate a few weeks after her death in 1982, and, without telling either of his brothers he slipped the slender volume with its fake leather cover into his pocket. The relentless advance of Alzheimer's had made it necessary to confine Hannah to a home. His brothers usually put it that way—in the passive voice. Rabin did not have the same luxury. After the fourth or fifth time she had been found wandering the streets, unable to locate her own apartment building, Rabin, his wife, and the last of Hannah's home nurses, a large, gentle Black woman named Elsa, had worked together to ease his mother into the car. Hannah might no longer recognize the difference between a one-dollar and a hundred-dollar bill, or be able to find the correct key for a lock, or successfully dial a phone number, but she understood the truth about this particular journey. On the half-hour ride to Mar Vista, she never stopped weeping. When Rabin stopped the car and said, as playfully as his choked throat would allow, *Mom, let's take a little walk,* she grabbed onto the back of the bucket seat of the Volkswagen Rabbit and held on to it with the strength of a football lineman while he alternately coaxed, cajoled, scolded, raged, and threatened. It was Elsa, in a voice low and reassuring, who talked Hannah into loosening her grip and going quietly into Marvis Acres.

The diary posed some problems for Rabin. One was with the family. Not Chaim Baer or David, who were much too preoccupied with the process of counting, cataloging, and evaluating Hannah's possessions, trying to determine which would be divided among the sons and which would be sold off—the brooms and dustpans, the bedclothes, the old refrigerator and the new vacuum cleaner; Lazar's double-breasted suits, which still hung in the closet; Hannah's forty-two pairs of shoes, including half a dozen with platforms that dated back to the late forties; the sterling silver; the German crystal glasses and dessert plates, which had been a wedding present; the nineteenth-century French inlaid piano; the small copy, on porcelain, of a hefty nude circled with flying *putti* by Cabanel that had been a winner at the Paris Salon of 1886; the antique Wedgwood vase that was similar to one in the Montreal Museum of Art; the Capa di Monte and Sèvre vases and candelabra that Lazar had bought *for a song* at estate sales in Montreal; the three sets of English bone china; and the hand-painted teacups Hannah had begun to collect on their honeymoon in New York more than fifty years before.

The major problem was with Aunt Lena in Providence. *Send it to me immediately,* she commanded over the phone in a peremptory tone that Rabin had never before heard in her voice. *I know your mother would not want you to read her diary!* She was probably right, but it was too late. Besides, Hannah was *his* mother and he was not about to surrender one of the few authentic documents (other than Adolph's published memoir) that he had to help construct the story of his family. Yet sending it to Aunt Lena might have made things easier. Up to this point the family story had been based on random scraps and fugitive sources, on personal memories, a few old letters, hasty conversations with distant cousins, taped interviews with his brothers, common family stories whose origins nobody could remember, and the contents of crumbling albums that contained more than half a century of photographs and other miscellaneous documents—bar mitzvah and wedding invitations; certificates of circumcision featuring pictures of the bearded rabbis who had performed the job; notices from the Selective Service System to report for physical examinations; diplomas from junior and senior high schools; clothing lists from summer camps; thank-you notes; birthday and anniversary cards; and newspaper clippings that described births, job promotions, illnesses, graduations, marriages, divorces, courtroom trials, and funerals.

Sources like these demanded creative interpretation, but any historian was bound to find a written document like a diary at once more solid and intractable. Daunting, too, since this one had been written by Rabin's mother more than a decade before he was born. The entries ran from June 2, 1923, to September 1, 1925, precisely the period covered in Rabin's still incomplete chapter Wild Hannah, the stormy months when the great love of her life, Julius, left Montreal to go to medical school in Paris and Hannah was swept off her feet by Lazar Rotenstein. Over the years his mother had so often talked of Julius that the outline of the story told in the diary presented few surprises. Had she passed on the details so well because she reread her own words? Or had Hannah simply never forgotten the events of that period? Babies, big houses, grand pianos, costly antiques, fancy vacations, mink coats, moving to California—nothing had been as important as those two years when she had lost a lover and gained a husband.

For years, Rabin worried over how to use the diary. Odd feelings were aroused by peeking into the fears, torments, and joys of a love story starring his teenage mother. It was a turbulent tale, a piece of high drama, with a plot more complex, stormy, and intense than the one she had told Rabin—and also with a larger cast of male characters. The diary begins with yearning for Julius, who is always addressed in the second person—*"U" left yesterday and already I feel the pangs of loneliness.* His departure from Montreal for a summer of work at a mountain resort is the reason she begins to write, and the falling tears and sadness of the early entries will continue long after his brief return to the city and his swift departure for France. Along with this absent lover (who doesn't write often enough, and what letters he does write are too short) and the very present Lazar Rotenstein, a number of other young men—George, Dave, Markus, Charlie, Bernard, Phillip, and Eddy—enter Hannah's life and fantasies with descriptions both favorable and detailed, this one for his eyes, that one for his intelligence, or income, or wit, or smoothness on the dance floor, or his suitability as a marriage companion.

Why does she choose Lazar? allow herself to be chosen? He begins talking marriage on their second date, but the first tiny expressions of love by Hannah for Lazar are not recorded until after the engagement party some months later. On January 4, the day of his formal proposal, she is already full of confusion, doubts, and fears that will last almost until the wedding day: *My soul is in perpetual torment, in a fever of indecision and unrest. . . . Must I marry some one who fits not into my scheme of thoughts. And is it thus ordained or am I master of my Fate?* Lazar is not the soulmate or teacher that Julius was, and when they are not rushing about to restaurants or to night clubs or sledding in the snowy country, he can seem a bit dull and lacking, but precisely what he lacks she can never specify. Her honest expressions of doubt make Hannah feel guilty, ashamed of herself, unworthy of Lazar. He seems so good, so devoted, so caring. When Hannah is sick with a bad flu, he sits by her bed every evening; when she spends an evening at home with the family, he calls to say goodnight. When Julius unexpectedly returns to Montreal in February and creates a huge scene, Hannah confesses everything to Lazar—and wonder of wonders, he proves to be totally unselfish about her past—*that is why I feel my love growing daily, hourly, minutely. . . . I don't want Lazar to find anything lacking in me. For him I must appear perfection.*

Only once does Hannah give vent to her full range of frustration and doubt. In mid-May 1924, two months after the engagement party when he presents her with a two-carat diamond ring, they have an awful quarrel: *Perhaps I have sold my birthright for a mess of pottage. Now I admit that at first I was dazzled by the false glitter of his money, by the big car, by the thoughts of a Baby Grand Piano in a beautiful home. Now I am left with my dreams shattered. . . . What am I going to do with a love like mine. He doesn't understand it, and appreciates it only as far as his very poor upbringing allows him to. If he would only have had the careful childhood "U" had, all would be different, and his intellect would have been far more highly developed. And his mother is to blame! She's the cause of his stunted growth, his unappeased education. L would have been wonderful if only he had a chance to expand and get away from the narrow environment. I can't respect a mother that willfully wrecks her own child's future. And the terrible pity of it is that the boy has the goods, and through lack of nourishment it's rotting away. Domineered all his life by an arrogant and unscrupulous brother, increasingly nagged by a scolding mother, life has not been too sweet a thing for him. Yet his nature has remained surprisingly sweet-tempered and calm.*

One of Lazar's attractions was his age and experience. When he mentions a former girlfriend, Hannah grows *obsessed with insane jealousy.* Yet it is nice to be with a man who knows his way around: *He's extremely broad minded, and I never feel that he thinks I am vulgar. It's nice to feel that way with a boy. Most men MAKE you feel your sex. But Lazar doesn't because his self-control is masterly and clean.* Four days before the engagement party on March 20, that self-control vanishes: *All my old cherished illusions have indeed gone smash—for the last shred absolutely was destroyed tonight. . . . What are men but soft flesh and blood, that yield, oh, ever so easily, yes yield and seduce too. When the truth of the matter dawned upon my virgin soul the overwhelming disgust was almost nauseating. . . . Oh, he forgets my age and explains nothing. . . . Oh why don't you tell me things, explain and teach me, because God knows, I am willing.*

Two days later, her mood has changed: *And it came to pass my revulsion turned into a vast, deep joy. . . . Ah. How I loved you last night. Lazar was exceedingly high strung last night and I delighted in his obvious passion with great glee. I have to see him in that mood for it awakens something fierce and primitive in me, and I long to be back in the ages where man took what belonged to him. His eyes smolder with deep hot fires, his body radiates unnatural heat, and the caresses he bestows on his equally passionate mate fans the flame to a heat almost beyond human endurance. . . . His suffering is intense, fearfully acute and nerve wracking yet never did I love you better than to see you in its throes. Yes, my joy is fiendish—or natural?* The next day she becomes the aggressor: *Tonight I felt fierce and utterly savage and I nearly bit poor Lazar to pieces in a frenzy of sudden passion, gusts that shook my frame with a ferocious lust. But oh, I felt fine, in the pink of condition, all ready for a killing.* The next week, when they stand opposite each other as Maid of Honor and Best Man at the wedding of Moishe and Ida, the physical has been transformed into the spiritual: *Under the canopy I felt it was all very solemn and beautiful. My heart felt so large that I thought it occupied my whole body. I was athrob with a great and holy love.*

In the upbeat weeks before the wedding on March 25, 1925, friends give Hannah four showers—kitchen, miscellaneous, personal, and linen—and she is the guest of honor at a bunch of formal afternoon teas. After the wedding night—*heavenly in its pure and spotless virginity. Lazar was simply perfection. Naturally we didn't sleep a wink—* they are off to New York for two weeks, staying at the Astor Hotel— *the bright lights dazzle me*—and taking in all the daytime tourist sites: Chinatown (*ugh—gruesome*), the Bronx Zoo (*great*), the Aquarium (*ain't Nature Grand?*), the Public Library at Fifth and Forty-second, the Woolworth Building (*wonderful*), the Automat (*how funny*), the subway (*takes my breath away*). At night it was a whirlwind of shows (*The Student Prince, Ziegfield Follies, Louis 14th, Rose Marie, White Cargo*) and cabarets: the Hippodrome, the Cotton Club (*the hottest nigger show in town*), and Club Alabam (*a very spicy review*).

Heartbroken to end her *precious beautiful honeymoon,* Hannah makes only three more entries in the diary. On April 24, their first-month anniversary, Lazar is in the hospital recovering from a hernia operation. On her twentieth birthday, June 7, she receives *a wonderful baby grand piano.* But the day is not one of pure joy: *Lazar had a serious accident the result of a bad temper. The tendon of his right hand was cut.* The final entry comes three months later after an apparent, oblique suggestion made by Lazar's mother that Hannah had not been a virgin when they married, and a subsequent quarrel between husband and wife. Never again in the following six decades will Hannah ever keep a diary, never again attempt to record in print the secrets of her heart. September 18, 1925, is some kind of ending, the day when life took over from words: *Lazar's mother is the most miserable wretch on earth. We had an awful quarrel with her last night. She said she forced Lazar to marry me, and she knows why— Oh God, why did I marry, and if marry at all, why any like him?! A cur that couldn't even stick up for me! I saw Eddie in the street. The love, the admiration that could have been mine. And then this with Lazar. Here I'm barely out of my teens and the suffering—the heartache that are mine I wish on* no *girl, however unfortunate.*

Grandma Sarah, looking the only way I can ever imagine she looked.

FIVE

The Afterthought

Jan. 25/24 I visited Mrs. Rotenstein last night again. She is lovely I think. Such a surprise.

Feb. 18th Monday Mrs. Rotenstein gave a party last night and Mama & Papa were there too. The dinner was delicious and so was everything else. Little Hymie is a darling kiddie and Frannie is an exceedingly sweet and lovable girl. Today . . . I went up there again for supper. Had a jolly time as we gathered in the kitchen. Ida and Moishe quarreled as usual and spoiled all my fun.

May 16th/25 Sat. Lazar and I had an awful quarrel. But he made up! Since then our understanding seems based on a firmer foundation. . . . What am I going to do with a love like mine. He doesn't understand it, and appreciates it only as far as his very poor upbringing allows him to. If he would only have had the careful childhood "U" had, all would be different, and his intellect would have been far more highly developed. And his mother is to blame! She's the cause of his stunted growth, his unappeased education. Lazar would have been wonderful if only he had a chance to expand and get away from the narrow environment. I can't respect a mother that willfully wrecks her own child's future.

Sept. 18th Lazar's mother is the most miserable wretch on earth. We had an awful quarrel with her last night. She said she forced Lazar to marry me, and she knows why—

FROM THE DIARY OF HANNAH KREISLER

*M*en! *They get to do everything, to go off to other countries, to migrate first, to spend their years in Paris, to run around with other women—and what did we get to do: to bake* progen *and make* mamaliga *and take care of the kids—for which we got little enough thanks at the time, and the result is that even now, decades later, nobody can see us very clearly and nobody can hear our voices—certainly not our grandsons, and not the men we lavished all our love upon, may they all rest in peace. No, they only want to tell about their grandfathers, swimming rivers, crossing oceans, gambling away their life's savings, jumping into bed with other women, sure, women who never grow old, who stay young, with sweet juicy bodies, women who are always making eyes and spreading their legs and telling their grandfathers* Ooh, you're such a mensch, *women who never have children and who never become grandmothers wearing those shapeless black dresses, women who are not handicapped by time, by accent, by having to clean a thousand bedpans of sick children, by having to prepare a million meals, by having to worry if their holy grandfathers will return from all those romantic places they've gotten themselves off to, those romantic adventures and scrapes with the law and illegal political groups aimed at saving the world that their darling grandsons will immortalize in poetry and prose, in history books and novels, and only once in a while will one of them get the slightest inkling, the tiniest hint that maybe, just maybe, those old women in the stiff and stilted photos, those women who won't smile because their teeth are gone and their arthritis makes it hard for them to sit up straight while the photographer is focusing his camera, oi* it takes so long, in the drafty studio, *those women who wonder what is the name of that odd, potted plant looming over her, a plant the likes of which she has never seen before and will never see again, those women who will hate the image that the camera will produce and will hate even more that their sons will exclaim,* It's you, Mama. It looks just like you, *and they will look at the stiff, grim old woman in the chair with the plant looming over her and think,* No. That's not me. That can't be me. I'm not that old, not that stiff, that foreboding, that grim. Where in this image is the love I feel for my sons and daughters and my grandsons and granddaughters? That woman in the picture could not have baked honey cake in love, you can see that, you can't see the *homentaschen* either, you can't see her saying Friday night prayers over the candles I have just lit, hand covering my eyes, the prayers that it should be all right for all *mein kinder,* for everyone's *kinder,* you can't see the fears she feels when her man left for foreign cities, you can't see the girl I was, the countryside I knew, the fields and streams, the grove of trees where he, who can remember his name, I was eleven, twelve and he was about to be bar mitzvah when our lips met and we promised to kiss only each other for the rest of our lives, such an important promise and I can't remember his name, the moon, the stars, the lives that I have touched. . . .

Me? I'm an afterthought. Vot den? No surprise that Rabin is like all Jewish men. Claims to honor women, to cherish them above all else. But when it comes to writing about the family he's only interested in his grandfather, Chaim Baer. No doubt he'll say it's because I'm too shadowy—no family stories about me, except that standard image, that one photo in the scrapbook of his mother, Hannah, that standard image of a grim old lady in black. The problem is that Hannah never liked me because I spoke my mind right out, told the truth even if it hurts (as it usually does), and her mother, Freda, hated me because she with her German words and dislike for garlic had to come to my apartment and speak in Yiddish and the result is that the image in the album isn't me but some distant friend of Hannah's mother. Has she forgotten or is it revenge for me pointing out that before the marriage to my Lazar she was not exactly pure as the snow on Mount Royal. There were once other photos of me when I was younger, and in a light dress, and smiling, and, if not pretty, at least full of a certain girlish charm. But my daughters-in-law never saw me that way. No. I was the old matriarch who kept their schoene *husbands tied to my apron strings.*

As if anyone could do anything with those two men—Moishe and Lazar, Lazar and Moishe. Just like their father, they were both impossible—stubborn and uncommunicative, and more interested in each other than anything else—including me. Imagine: not a single story will Lazar or Moishe pass on about me. No wonder. Never did they ask about my past. But twenty years after Chaim Baer died, when they were already married and living in big houses in Westmount among all the goyim, *thinking they were so smart, so far from the Main, they sometimes would, when they stopped in the afternoon to see how I was, and drink a single schnapps rather than a cup of coffee, ask about their father's life in Odessa, or Tetscani, or his famous year in Paris—a year that I, for one, could have done without. All very fine for him, drinking wine and gallivanting around with French women and rarely sending a word to tell me he was safe, but who had to take care of those seven wild kids while he was off seeing the world?*

With those two men such questions seemed to be part of measuring themselves against their father's progress in life. With Rabin, the questions must mean something else. Yet if he can find Chaim Baer so heroic, you'd think it might occur to him, at least for an instant, to wonder about the woman who married this romantic figure. Maybe she wasn't always that dour, heavy-set woman dressed in black, seated in an overstuffed chair. Maybe she had dreams, hopes, desires that are also worthy of recovering. Maybe she did not want to spend her life in a remote, muddy Romanian village, raising kids, milking the cow, preparing meals, sewing their clothes (even though he was the tailor, but you think Mr. Fancy Pants would make clothes for his kids—well, he did, but only for the boys and only for their bar mitzvah suits). If my grandson is so smart, maybe he could even make something of the fact that I, too, did some traveling; that the fact I was Polish, and had somehow gotten myself to Romania (however much a mistake that might be) at least meant that Grandma Sarah is more than a shadow but a flesh and blood woman with an interesting story to tell, a story that for all his supposed interest in the family, will never be told. Well, why not. Stories are for them, the men. They don't believe in things unless they can be wrapped into words. Kaina hora, they are our burden and our joy, so let them have their stories. They need them more than we do. Only they should be well, keep dry, eat regular, come home, call or stop by once in a while, and keep the bed warm—what more can a woman ever ask?

Lazar and Moishe, hurrying somewhere, during World War II.

SIX

Transylvania Sank

All About A Little Brown Dog
Skippy's Family. By Stephen W. Meader. McLeod; $2.50

This is the true life story of a little brown dog named Skippy. He was found and lived in a town in New Jersey the seventeen years of his life.

The book tells of adventures he had, adventures that might happen to any dog. He had so many that it seems incredible that so many things could happen to one dog.

In places the book holds you in suspense. Frequently Skippy got hopelessly lost and sometimes it seemed that he might never be found.

When Skippy was about thirteen years old another dog came to live in the same house. He was named Misto. Misto and Skippy had many happy adventures together.

The book is adventure after adventure from the first page to the last.

At seventeen years of age Skippy died. But he was never forgotten by the family. I found the book very easy to read and recommend it to boys and girls my age.　　　　　—Rabin A. Rotenstein, age 9

THE MONTREAL GAZETTE, NOV. 17, 1945

The third and final summer that the Rotenstein family stayed in Farmer Belisle's cottage close to Trout Lake was the summer that Rabin's eldest brother, Chaim Baer, stopped telling his famous story about vampires. In previous years he had regularly recited the tale at bedtime, in a shadowy room lit only by a kerosene lamp, his voice so haunted and ghoulish that Rabin would huddle beneath the covers, terrified, until his father, Lazar, would come into the room and say, *Stop scaring your brother. There's no such thing as vampires and I ought to know: I'm from Romania.* The terror would last after Lazar shooed Chaim Baer out of the room, kissed Rabin goodnight, and darkened the lamp, but the details of the story vanished. Soon after his brother stopped the telling, Rabin could recall nothing save for the single image of a white body with two small puncture wounds in the neck lying in a coffin and the closing words: *And Transylvania sank beneath the waves!*

Imagine a land (Rabin would think years later) famed everywhere for a single figure—a bloodsucker named Dracula. Like many great people, Dracula was at once historical and fictional, with the fictional personage—as usual—by far the better known. The historical Prince Dracul (*Devil* in Romanian) was Vlad the Third, sometime ruler of the province of Wallachia in the middle of the fifteenth century. Rather less of a humanist than the fictional Dracula created by Bram Stoker, Vlad was in his day widely known for generous, and unusual, gifts. One year he sent several bags full of heads, noses, and ears to the king of Hungary to put under the Christmas tree. He also took an interest in the fledgling science of statistics. At the end of the campaign along the Danube in 1462, Vlad noted in his journal that his army had killed *23,884 Turks and Bulgars, without counting those whom we burned in homes or whose heads were not cut off by our soldiers.*

Prince Dracul's real specialty began at the rear end of the body. With equal parts affection and fear, he was referred to all over Christendom (and in parts of the Muslim world) as The Impaler. On such a scale did he pierce people with wooden stakes (rounded at the end so that the entrails would not be torn too badly and death not come too quickly) that the historian is inclined to suggest that the Prince must have held shares in the lumber industry. Twenty thousand Turks got the treatment on a single afternoon in 1471, following the Battle of Giurgiu. For such excess, Dracula had a good excuse. Months of warfare with the troops of Sultan Muhammad II had left him woefully short of sleep, and to take prisoners was to risk long nights of lamentations in Turkish, a language whose sound he despised.

No more than Rabin's father despised bats, creatures that—had his hands been quick enough—he would not have hesitated to impale. Lazar's skirmishes with the creatures took place in the summer, in the same cottages where Chaim Baer told and then stopped telling his vampire story. When a bat made the mistake of flying into the cottage and began to bang against walls and ceilings, Lazar would carefully remove his wire rim glasses and don a rubber shower cap in the belief that *Bats like to pull out your hair* (a statement that drew long hoots and jeers from his sons, who thought that Lazar's vastly receding hairline and thin, graying hair constituted, for all practical purposes, baldness). Grabbing up a long-handled broom, blind as a you-know-what, Lazar lurched from room to room, swinging and bumping, knocking down pitchers, shattering globes, tripping over chairs, yelling all the while like a madman or—Rabin would realize decades later—a kung fu warrior. Eventually a blow would find the creature. Before he dropped his fallen adversary into the garbage can, Lazar would show his children the tiny, frail animal that up close was no more frightening than the mice they regularly caught in spring-loaded traps baited with bits of white Canadian cheddar.

Lazar might claim birth in a rural village named Tetscani, but to his children he always seemed a creature of the city. Occasionally he told stories of the grape harvests of his youth, but the cows, pigs, chickens, or stands of ripening corn of rural Quebec never drew his attention. Each and every country morning when the rooster crowed, he cursed aloud. When others went berrying, Lazar stayed in the cottage to do crossword puzzles. When he appeared at the lakeshore in a bathing suit, he rarely did much more than dip a toe into the water. One particularly hot day, when he rowed with the kids to the raft and then slipped into the lake to cool off, the family Airedale, Prince, who would usually watch us swim with a bemused expression that suggested such watery exertions were fine for lesser species, suddenly leaped from the raft in an apparent attempt to save his master. For a few moments, the frantic dog seemed to forget that he had paws, not hands. Ten minutes later Lazar was being rushed in a taxi to a doctor in St. Agathe for tetanus shots. The bandages over his back and arms were not removed for a week.

One Friday afternoon Lazar arrived at Trout Lake with a car full of brand-new fishing gear—fancy flannel shirts, rods and reels, boxes of flies, sport hats, and rubber boots. *We Rotenstein men are going fishing,* he announced, and the next day he packed David and Chaim Baer into the car—Hannah insisted Rabin was too young to go along—and the three of them disappeared into the woods for a week. Did they bring home fish? You should live so long. It rained, the boat capsized, Chaim Baer almost drowned, David got his famous croup cough, and Lazar sprained his wrist from casting the wrong way with his rod. They came home exhausted and sick, with Lazar in one of his foul humors. At the end of the summer, the fishing gear was heaped into a corner of the basement, never again to be used or mentioned.

For Rabin the country had other terrors: Bees, wasps, and black hornets that inevitably nested in bushes with the juiciest of berries, and—at the end of the summer—allowed him to brag to friends back in Montreal about surviving twenty-seven stings and three shots administered with a needle two feet long. Cows: that late one afternoon chased the chubby, short-legged lad all the way down from a hillside pasture to the barn. (*Dummy, you were in their path. They were hurrying home for milking,* said David.) Green apples: that produced a dangerous stomach ache when you ate twenty or so directly from the tree. Buttermilk: a nasty surprise the first time you pull a bottle from the ice box after playing baseball and take a huge swallow expecting sweet milk. Fresh vegetables: except for corn. And Aunt Sybil: a practical nurse whose position empowered her during wartime to use whatever means possible to throw off enemy spies, among whom she apparently numbered Rabin. The evening she appeared in his bedroom, he instinctively knew she was there to tear the bandages from his stings. *No,* she insisted, *I only want to make sure they are still on all right.* Would he ever trust anyone again? They came off with a sharp ripping sound that blended neatly into his scream. Aunt Sybil was smiling. In the middle of the night, Rabin went down to the dock and untied the rowboat belonging to Sybil and Schloime. It took them three days of searching along the lakeshore to find it.

Lazar might never take his sons horseback riding or on hikes, but every Saturday he would drive them to the movies at one of the two theaters in St. Agathe, the Alhambra and the Roxy. Since it was illegal for anyone under sixteen to attend films in Quebec, the fun was spiced with the danger of a possible *raid*. Once in the middle of a show at the Roxy, the manager and two ushers came running down the aisle, waving flashlights and yelling for kids to exit the theater by the doors next to the screen. Sixty youngsters stood in the parking lot behind the theater, each wondering: *Will I be arrested? Will I miss dinner?* After the manager came out to say, *The coast is clear,* they were outraged to find that the film had not been stopped during their absence.

Rabin had heard Chaim Baer tell the vampire story for years, but only during the third summer when they stayed at the Farmer Belisle's did he specifically ask to hear it. And that was just the summer when Chaim Baer refused to tell the story anymore. Later Rabin would wonder as much about his desire to hear the story as about his brother's reluctance to tell it. Perhaps both had to do with the times. Vampires were abroad in the world, and the rise and fall of his brother's voice mingled with the radio voices that Lazar insisted on listening to every evening while they ate. The menacing tone often made his father angry, and the boy would leave the kitchen for the coolness of the evening porch. After dinner, the sky was dark blue. When it got black, they might see the northern lights, and the sight would make everyone forget about words like *fascist*, *Nazi*, and *deadandwounded*.

The three years they lived at Trout Lake were not only the years of the War, they were the years of the War Effort, which seemed to be a wholly separate enterprise. Neither touched Rabin very deeply. None of his older cousins or young uncles were taking part in the war, at least not until the day when Uncle Mendel showed up on Vendome driving a jeep. Before this, the only soldiers Rabin had seen were those in mud-colored uniforms parading down Sherbrooke in December. Uncle Mendel parked the jeep in the driveway. He had a cigar in his mouth, and he wore a mud-colored uniform. His collar was unbuttoned and his necktie and soft cap lay on the backseat, next to the small wooden crate stamped *Johnny Walker* that he lifted carefully and carried toward the house.

Rabin and his friends crowded around the vehicle. Uncle Mendel was quite a guy. Lazar met his brother at the door and slapped him on the back. When Mendel came out of the house a few minutes later, he took Rabin for a ride. *Where to, sport?* he asked, as they bounced up Vendome. *Uncle Moishe's. Let's get Sheila.* They raced along Notre Dame de Grace, and Rabin asked his uncle how long he had been in the army. Mendel ignored the question and, with the cigar stuck in the corner of his mouth, answered: *Winston Churchill— You know Churchill, don't you? When he was in town, who do you think was his driver? Your favorite uncle, that's who! But not in this jeep. No sir. Churchill had a big, long limousine and a case of whiskey in the trunk, and he kept sipping right from a bottle all day long. And you know what he told me? He told me I was the best damn driver he had ever had. He told me to look him up after the war if I ever needed anything!*

Nobody was home at Uncle Moishe's, so Mendel zipped up and down the hills of Westmount for a while before taking Rabin home. When he saw his uncle a few weeks later, Mendel was wearing a chef's apron and standing behind the counter of a restaurant way out on Decarie, past Blue Bonnet racetrack, on the way toward the mountains. It was late afternoon. Rabin was eating his favorite dish, one you could not get at home, hash and poached eggs. Hannah was drinking coffee and smoking. Lazar was sipping something from a glass and saying, *Yeah. You'll do all right here. With the Laurentian Highway almost finished, this should be a great spot.* Rabin kept asking, *Where's the jeep? What happened to your uniform?* Mendel never answered. *They can't keep a Rotenstein in the army,* Lazar said.

Part of the War Effort had to do with keeping quiet; part with buying stamps. Posters in school and all over the city urged you to keep your mouth shut so that the enemy would not learn secrets. This was easy to do since school kids neither knew any secrets nor had any idea what kind of a secret the enemy might like to know. The stamps cost ten cents, and you bought two each Friday at school and pasted them in a book. Ten years later you would get twenty-five dollars back from the government for each full book. This was a better deal than the one for the stamps with pictures of little trees on them that Rabin bought every week at the end of Sunday school class at the Sha'ar Hashomayim. The return on these, the rabbi explained, was the *mitzvah* that came from contributing to the efforts of those pioneers who were reclaiming the sandy land of your forebears. Someday you would go to Palestine and see your name on a plaque in front of each tree for which you had paid.

The War Effort also had to do with food. Urged on by teachers and public posters and radio announcements, Rabin insisted over Hannah's objections on digging up the backyard to plant a Victory Garden. His efforts didn't much help the Allied cause. The tiny tomato plants he had Lazar buy from a nursery soon withered, the cucumbers never bloomed, the carrots were white and shriveled. Only the radishes grew in profusion, but everyone in the family found them too bitter except for Lazar, who crunched them while saying, *You think these are bitter? In Romania the radishes were so bitter that even the Gypsies wouldn't steal them!*

On the day that ration books were first issued, the family crowded around the breakfast table, looking at the brand-new booklets with the brightly colored red, blue, and green stamps. Hannah held one out and wailed as she turned the pages: *A pound of meat per person a week . . . a pound of butter a month . . . a pound of sugar . . .* Lazar gestured impatiently: *Don't worry. Don't worry.* A few days later when Rabin wanted to see the stamps again, the books were gone. *Don't you need them? How will we eat?* His father shook his head: *We gave them all to Selzer, the butcher. He'll take good care of us.* And so he did. Every morning of the war, the Rotensteins covered their breakfast bagels with thick layers of real butter and every evening they consumed huge portions of meat—steaks, chops, roasts of beef and lamb. At the end of each dinner, they never failed to enjoy Hannah's sweet, buttery home-baked desserts: the chocolate cakes, berry pies, and sugar-topped cookies called *kuchel*. At noon every day, their Airedale, Prince, was fed a pound and a half of ground round steak.

Gas rationing was a more serious matter. Every car had to have a large official sticker in the lower right-hand corner of the windshield, designating the category to which the driver belonged. The highest rating, *AAA*, was reserved for government officials and high military officers. *AA* went to engineers, doctors, and dentists, like the father of Arthur Stampleman. *A* was given to workers at defense plants like Mr. Wolfe, accountants like Mitchell Klein's father, pharmacists like Mr. Held. *B* went to the father of Morton Schwartz, a junkman who had recently taken to calling himself a scrap metal dealer. When Lazar Rotenstein came home from the government gasoline office, the sticker on his windshield had a bright red *D*.

Daddy, whined Rabin. *You won't have enough gas to get to Lachine,* said Chaim Baer. *Did they make up a new category for you alone?* asked David. *Category, schmategory,* said Lazar. *They wanted to give me an* E *but I told them I had to drive my feeble-minded sons to school.* When Uncle Moishe showed up with the same red *D* on the windshield of his Buick, the pain eased a bit, but the embarrassment of driving with his father did not end until months later when the sticker itself began to weather and fade. Yet the reality, as Rabin would later come to understand about life, rarely had anything to do with the truth on a label. Not for a single day during the War and the War Effort did the Rotenstein family ever lack for gasoline. Nor for a moment did Lazar curb his love of driving. During the summer months he drove up to the mountains one, two, three times a week. His favorite story in those years was the one about how, when buying gas in rural Quebec, he held out ration coupons only to have them waved away with the comment, in a heavy French accent: *Those are for the Jews in Montreal!*

Not everything about Jews was funny the summer Chaim Baer stopped telling the story about Transylvania. Names of uncles and aunts and cousins that Rabin had never before heard—names like *Sascha* and *Ziggy*—were spoken in hushed tones by Moishe and Ida, and by Auntie Lena and Uncle Paul when they visited from Providence, and by Uncle Elliot and Joan when they arrived from New York with a two-layer box of Whitman's Sampler chocolates for each of the kids. Sometimes adults would mutter *It's not good for the Jews* when they listened to the radio. An election was about to happen—

Rabin was old enough to know that, and old enough to know that he was supposed to like a party named the CCF. But he preferred Le Bloc Populaire because of the way announcers boomed out the party name, and he liked the way crowds cheered in the background when speakers roared their message in a language he could not understand. If it was *populaire* there must be a good reason, but not one good enough to convince his father. Rabin was old enough to know that too, and he kept his political preferences to himself.

When Lazar was not in the mountains during the summer, he was in the city sweating over the problems of General Metal Company. Rabin's father was always looking for a chance to go legit, and General Metal was one of those businesses he had acquired when somebody defaulted on a debt. Like the others, General Metal became in his mind more than a respectable front, yet Lazar had no touch for legal endeavors. A metal company seemed especially promising. It was wartime and surely the government would need things made out of metal. The manager of the factory, Pietr Shultz, had geared up for Dutch ovens. *An army marches on its stomach,* he told Lazar, and what better way to keep soldiers happy than cooking things in Dutch ovens. Schultz was, Lazar assumed, Dutch. But just to make sure, he asked him straight out, the week he moved into the factory. Two years later, General Metal had yet to land a government contract. Much as he hated to mix enterprises, Lazar turned for help to a government official who laid a bet with him every week. The answer came back: *You'll never get a contract as long as you have a German manager.* An angry Lazar confronted an equally angry manager:

I thought you said you were Dutch.

No. I told you: I bin deutsch.

The third summer on the Belisle farm, Rabin's two brothers were not very nice. At the corner store, they would not play catch or Ping Pong with him but instead hung around the jukebox with some girls named Zelda and Shelley listening to Peggy Lee sing *Get out of here and get me some money too, like the other men do.* When Rabin told his father that he wanted to learn how to ride a two-wheel bike, Lazar turned the job over to Chaim Baer and David, who were annoyed by the order to spend time with their kid brother. On the morning they taught him how to mount a bicycle and how to balance and how to pedal, they neglected to teach him something even more important: how to dismount. Rabin began that first ride all by himself, feeling proud and grown-up, but when his legs began to tire and he said, *Help me off,* his brothers screamed with laughter and danced about the yard sticking their fingers in their ears and making faces. He steered toward them, but they dodged away, and when Rabin began to shout (only it sounded more like a squeal), *Help me, help—get me off,* Chaim Baer and David raced off behind the barn, leaving the youngster to sob and wobble and, in an act of desperation, to end the ride by crashing into the gazebo. A little iodine took care of the scratches on his legs and elbows, but neither Hannah nor Aunt Sybil had anything for the marks on his heart.

Years later Rabin would recall the exact time when Chaim Baer stopped telling the story about vampires. It was not long after David, over the objections of Hannah, decided to swim across Trout Lake with a couple of friends. They were going to do it the long way, which was more than a mile, and they all refused to have anyone in their families row alongside them *just in case.* All afternoon the family lingered by the phone, awaiting a call from the grocery store on the other side of the lake. The next weekend, a young woman who couldn't swim fell out of a boat and sank. They dragged the lake for days, then they brought in a diver in a heavy rubber suit and a glass and metal helmet, but they never found the body. Rabin would long remember standing on a hill at twilight, between trees that were already black, looking at the silver lake and hearing the throb of the compressor on a barge sending air to the diver down below. Hannah held one of his hands and Lazar the other. Chaim Baer and David were silhouettes along the shore. Rabin would never know why he picked that night to ask his brother to tell the story of Transylvania, the story he would never tell again.

Hannah, Lazar, and the author on Miami Beach in January 1940. I am apparently armed to defend myself against any Germans who may attempt to bother us on the voyage we are about to make to Cuba.

SEVEN

Lower California, Here We Come

ALL EXCEPT 3 OF NAZI WAR CHIEFS GUILTY;
GOERING, HESS, VON RIBBENTROP CONVICTED;
SCHACHT, VON PAPEN, FRITZSCHE ACQUITTED

---

12 NAZI WAR LEADERS SENTENCED TO BE HANGED;
GOERING HEADS LIST OF THOSE TO DIE BY OCT. 16;
HESS GETS LIFE, SIX OTHERS ORDERED TO PRISON

ARMY ASKS A YEARLY DRAFT
OF 726,000 YOUTHS 18 TO 20
6 MONTHS ACTIVE TRAINING

TRUMAN URGES PRICE CURBS,
INDUSTRIAL PEACE AND RISE
IN OUTPUT TO AVOID CRASH

TRUMAN AGAIN PRODS BRITAIN
ON 100,000 PALESTINE VISAS;
BACKS JEWISH STATE PLAN

TAFT CONDEMNS
HANGING FOR NAZIS
AS UNJUST VERDICT

DEWEY BIDS BRITAIN
OPEN UP PALESTINE
TO IMMIGRANTS NOW

**SMUTS AT PARLEY
WARNS THE NATIONS
OF EAST-WEST RIFT**

**BARUCH OPPOSES
SCRAPPING BOMBS
BEFORE ATOM PACT**

**CHAMBER OF COMMERCE OPENS CAMPAIGN
TO OUST REDS IN U.S. POSTS**

**FREEDOM OF DANUBE VOTED
OVER RUSSIAN OBJECTIONS;
RUMANIA PACT DRAFT PASSES**

**BULGARIAN TREATY VOTES,
GREEK BORDER UNDECIDED;
U.S. AID PLEDGED TO ATHENS**

HEADLINES FROM THE *NEW YORK TIMES*, OCT. 1–12, 1946
(DURING THE ROTENSTEIN JOURNEY ACROSS THE U.S.)

As if to prove my father's point about the move, it snowed on October 1, 1946, the day we left Montreal. He had convinced me to abandon my friends by promising that in California he would buy a fifty-foot yacht and sail down the coast to Honolulu. He had promised my brother, David, who had just graduated from Montreal High School, that he could enroll at the famed University of Lower California. Evidently my eldest brother, Chaim Baer, had a better sense of geography than either David or me, for he chose to stay behind and work at selling subscriptions for the *Montreal Gazette*. Not much of a job for the acknowledged *genius* of the family, but then it wasn't a real job but only a cover story to protect a ten-year-old brother—me. Like all of my uncles and male cousins and even my grandfather, the Hebrew teacher, Chaim Baer went to work in the numbers.

It could not have been easy. Chaim Baer was neither athletic nor brave nor particularly good at mathematics. His *genius* was largely verbal and musical. The combination had made him a poor student (too smart for the teachers to handle) and a pretty fair entertainer—but an unemployed entertainer. When he refused the scholarship to Juilliard and dropped out of private composition classes with the conductor of the Montreal Philharmonic, my father, recognizing spite when it was (or so he thought) directed at him, sent word out to all the night club and bar owners in the English-speaking part of Montreal—that anyone who hired his son would have to answer to him. Lazar might be no Godfather, but he had been around the rackets long enough to carry more than a little weight in the entertainment world.

My father's shaky sense of geography was understandable enough. Aside from the Hebrew study necessary for bar mitzvah, he had attended school for a total of six weeks. At this point he was the most educated member of his family—indeed, perhaps the most learned soul in Tetscani, a tiny rural community in Moldavia. Yanked from the classroom by his father, Chaim Baer, Lazar was set to work assisting in the tailor shop and helping with the gardens, the cows, and the goats. Those six weeks were perhaps the most important of his life. They gave him a taste for reading, learning, and the arts that was never shown by either of his two brothers or five sisters. All his life, the written word seemed to inflame in Lazar certain notions of romance and adventure. It was one thing for brother Mendel, the baby, to run away to sea as a teenager, but who other than Lazar would, at the age of forty—or forty-four—leave a good business and a secure position in the community for the unknown world of the United States at its farthest point—Lower California!

The snow that cast an air of gloom over our departure also delayed it. The previous day the temperatures had been in the eighties, so naturally all the sweaters were packed at the bottom of the trunk and chains for the car were nowhere to be found. We had to borrow a set belonging to Cousin Hymie—along with Chaim Baer, he and Shirley were the only ones there to see us off. David had already taken a train west to enroll at the university, and we had said our good-byes to Moishe's family the night before at a dinner at Ruby Foo. This new restaurant out on Decarie—no need to drive east to the Main for dinner anymore—had in recent months become everyone's favorite. The name and decor might be Chinese, and the jukebox might feature Frank Sinatra ballads rather than *Romania, Romania, Romania,* but the food at Ruby Foo, managed by one Abe Silverstein, was not much different from Moishe's steak house. Only here, before getting to the steaks, you ate egg rolls, sweet spare ribs, and almond chicken instead of chopped liver mixed with fried onions.

Everyone was dressed up, but it was not a happy occasion. The men wore dark suits and neckties, the women, dark, beaded dresses, upswept hair, and platform shoes, and my mother sported a pillbox hat that she did not remove during the meal. Sheila and I threw the cherries from our Shirley Temples at each other and, after Moishe roared at us to stop, kept poking each other in the ribs and giggling. Ida drank a bunch of martinis and started in on Hannah: *So you're gonna get away from all the Romanians at last, eh? Good-bye* mamaliga, *hello Hollywood.*

Moishe interrupted: *Shaa, Ida. Enough.*

You think you can find more people in California who prefer Chopin to poker?

Ida, you've had enough.

It was the wrong thing for him to say.

You, Mr. Wiseguy. You're so happy your kid brother's deserting you! So tell me, what else have you talked about for the past six months!

Listen, Moishe began . . .

Waiter. Another martini.

Ida, said Lazar. *It's not so far. You can fly coast to coast now. I'll be back. You can come visit. You've always liked the sun.*

Sure, sure, you'll be back, but you'll never be here again—you know what I mean?

Gusts of wind blow wet gray snow as Lazar steps on the ignition and roars the engine of the large, black Packard sedan, just the kind of car favored by movie gangsters who are about to meet with the leaders of another gang to divvy up some turf. *Six years new,* Lazar bragged when it came out of the shop the week before, the engine overhauled, the original paint job polished to a high gloss, the pinstriped, gray velvet upholstery soft and clean, the sidewalls of the new black-market tires dazzling white. Close to midday the Packard pulls to a halt on St. Mark's Street. Grandma and Grandpa stand in front of their apartment building. Lazar glances at his watch and mutters, *I've got to be in California by Christmas,* but Hannah, determined to say a proper good-bye, drags the two of us inside. The kettle is boiling. Good-bye consists of drinking two cups of tea with milk and eating two slices of Freda's leaden honey cake. Hannah and Freda work to keep the conversation lively. Half a dozen times I promise to be a good boy, to study Hebrew, and write letters often (in English). The men are uncomfortably silent, the kind of silence in which Adolph usually stands up, puts on a hat, and leaves the house. Now he remains seated, a broad, unconvincing smile pasted on his wide face.

So we'll take the train and come visit you soon, says Freda. *Won't we, Adolph.*

Aaach, says Adolph, with either satisfaction or disinterest in his voice. *Lazar, maybe you need a schnapps. Keep you warm.*

For the first time since coming indoors, my father gives the semblance of a smile: *For the road.*

· · ·

Only when they left his grandparents' did it really hit Rabin that they were leaving Montreal. The figures of Adolph and Freda had just vanished around the corner when he knew something was at an end, and suddenly he wanted to see lots of things so that in California he would remember what they looked like—St. Catherine Street, with its narrow trolley; the window displays at Morgan's and Eaton's; the Sun Life Building, the tallest in Canada; the Holland Building on Sherbrooke, owned by his father and Moishe; the campus of McGill University; the Blue Bird Barber Shop on Bleury; Fletcher's Field; the long toboggan slide on Mount Royal; the ski jump on Cotes des Neiges; the swans in La Fontaine Park; their old houses on Vendome and Sunnyside, and the mansion on Upper Belmont, sold when he was two years old, the site of his earliest memories: the sun is so bright he cannot open his eyes—the scene recorded for posterity, brown on white, by some anonymous professional photographer—he is in Lazar's arms, a chubby two-year-old in a jumper—while David and Chaim Baer, wearing dark shorts, white shirts, and bow ties mug at the camera.

Daddy, drive down St. Catherine Street.

No time to lose, says Lazar. *Got to be in New York by noon tomorrow.*

DADDY!

Oh, all right.

They sped down St. Catherine so fast that the store windows were a blur, then headed toward the river. Hannah was silent. Rabin pressed his face to the window. The skyline of Montreal under a streaky gray sky fell away, and they crossed the river on the Cartier Bridge.

You call that honey cake, said Lazar. *In a hundred years you couldn't teach a Litvak to bake.*

We were the only car at the Rouse's Point border station. Lazar fumed while American customs officials mulled the question of whether someone importing a 1940 Packard into the United States had to pay duties. *I'm not importing it. It's for me. I need a car to get around in California,* Lazar said over and over, his voice rising a bit more in pitch at each repetition. The customs officer was icy: *Mr. Rotenstein—we'll decide what* American *law says.* As time passed, Lazar's fear and fury rose in equal proportions. Did they know about the time he was turned back at Cleveland? Or about the conviction of Polly's husband for bootlegging? To his family in the waiting room, Lazar raged, *Haven't they got anything better to do?*

You and your ideas, said Hannah. *Nobody in his right mind would drag a family across the country in an old car.*

They don't make cars like this any more, said Lazar.

After an hour, American law—it turned out—agreed with Lazar's interpretation. *Bureaucrats,* he said, as they drove into northern New York. It was familiar country. Small white towns on shining lakes emerged out of thick forest. A gas station, a grocery store, a church, guest houses and inns, some with signs saying *Closed for the Winter,* rowboats turned upside down on narrow, sandy beaches, empty rafts rocking on the silvery water. Only a few people on the streets or beaches, huddled in their sweaters and coats. One lake, surrounded by black woods, was so big you could not see to the farther shore. *Champlain*, said Lazar. To Rabin the name brought images from history books: Indians taking scalps, Redcoats, struggles of stalwart Canadians against American rebels. In the town of Schroon Lake, Lazar slowed and waved at a large hotel, surrounded by porches, very white against a flat, broad expanse of vivid green lawn: *That's where your mother and I stayed before you were born.* It looked like a nice place to stay.

In Albany a jeweler's convention had filled the hotels, and all three of them had to sleep in one terrible room in a hotel named the New Kenmore—*I'd hate to see the old Kenmore,* said Lazar—where the floors rolled like the sea and the hallways smelled of stale corn beef and cabbage. This was an omen. It was to be a trip, to hear Lazar tell it, of terrible rooms and worse meals. Everywhere they stopped there was a convention: Middle Atlantic States Dentists in Wheeling, Indiana Insurance Salesmen in Indianapolis, agricultural implement dealers in Oklahoma City, Anasazi Indian Chiefs in Tucumcari, Southwest Loggers in Flagstaff, and Oklahoma Hog-Callers in Vinita, population 1,145. In St. Louis the World Series was in progress—Cards against the Red Sox—and prices were triple the rates listed in Lazar's guide from the Quebec Auto Club. In Amarillo a tornado had destroyed most of the local accommodations, with the same result. Someplace in the desert of New Mexico, a highly recommended inn (*where they throw you out*—Lazar) was no more than a pile of charred ruins. *Burned 'bout ten years ago,* said the ancient woman in the small general store, apparently the sole resident of the town. It was dusk, a red desert afterglow in the enormous sky silhouetting a gas pump, a dry pump. *Hasn't worked in years,* she said. Lazar, who has been in too much of a hurry to fill up after lunch, was almost out of gas. The subsequent hundred miles to Gallup were the most tense of the trip.

Bad rooms meant that Lazar never got a good night's sleep, but that was nothing new. For almost four decades, apparently ever since departing from Romania as a twelve-year-old, his sleep had been fitful. Yet every morning he had something to blame for his sleeplessness—leaky faucets, noisy coffee shops, rude guests, loud trucks on the highway. Such rooms were due to one of Lazar's rules of the road—never take the first accommodations you see. Which meant that he often passed up perfectly nice places in anticipation of palatial rooms that never did materialize. This practice went along with his rule about never eating in hotels, and never even asking people who owned, managed, or worked in hotels where to eat, because they were no doubt in league with various cronies and relatives, all of whom owned bad and expensive restaurants. With regard to food, Lazar was an offbeat kind of democrat. *Ask a local* was his motto. Across the United States, various gas station attendants, grocery clerks, or pedestrians were startled to find themselves confronted by a short, thickset man with rimless glasses, who asked: *Where do you like to eat?* The result was often a meal that left Lazar with an upset stomach, but he never questioned the procedure.

Dinner and breakfast in the New Kenmore were much the same: ham and eggs, which was fine with Rabin, who never got to eat ham at home. Not that the family was kosher. But Hannah had her own dietary laws, laws that seemed to have to do more with language than with food. Anything was OK to eat as long as certain words were not used to describe it. Bacon was a staple of the breakfast table, and country sausage was a regular treat. But anything that could be described by the words *pork* was strictly forbidden. No pork roast or chops, no pork fried rice in Chinese restaurants. The same went for *ham,* except for hamburgers, which were OK. But no ham sandwiches, no ham and eggs, though a club sandwich containing ham would be OK if you did not mention the contents aloud.

Lazar agreed to breakfast in a hotel *just this once* because he was *in a hurry.* Such a hurry that he did not see the other driver shoot out of traffic just as he was pulling out of the hotel parking lot. The scrape was agonizing; the left front fender of the Packard would never look so new again. Shouts, fists wave, and a policeman strolls over and tips his hat. A call *downtown* is necessary to determine if Canadian insurance is valid in New York. Half an hour wasted to find out the answer is yes. *I told them so,* Lazar shouted at Hannah and Rabin as they left Albany. *I know the States better than the natives do.*

Breakfast had to last a long time, so it was good that Rabin had eaten Hannah's ham and most of her two eggs and toast. Lazar had an appointment in Manhattan at two o'clock—which meant no stops at all, not for the bathroom, not for food, not for sight-seeing. While they waited in Albany for the policeman to find out about the insurance, Rabin was sent to the toilet three times. Half an hour out of the city, Rabin said: *I have to go.*

Impossible. It's too soon, said Lazar. He was gripping the steering wheel with white knuckles, passing all the other cars on the highway.

Really, Daddy, I've GOT to go!

Rabin, you've got to be a big boy. We can't stop now, we've just started.

Rabin began to bound up and down on the backseat: *Got to go. Got to go. Got to go.*

Lazar, said Hannah. *Your son's got to go.*

For Christ's sake. We just got on the road. We haven't gotten anywhere yet!

California, said Hannah, and burst into tears. Lazar began to slow down. *Okay, I'll pull over and you can go in the bushes along the road.*

Not number one, Daddy. I've got to go number two.

At a Texaco station on the outskirts of Poughkeepsie, Rabin sat on the toilet for a long time. The bathroom was white and clean, just like home. Just like home used to be, since right now they did not have a home. Poughkeepsie—there was something about the name that he liked. He imagined people in Poughkeepsie lived in neat homes and their daddies took them to baseball games on Sundays, double-headers, while their moms stayed home and made roasts for dinner. In Montreal, Lazar had never taken Rabin to a ball game. He paid for the tickets, but taking him to Delormier Downs was David's job, even to the doubleheader on his tenth birthday, when the Royals beat Syracuse twice and Jackie Robinson got six hits, including a homer. Rabin liked Jackie Robinson. Of course he was *supposed* to like him—his brothers and Lazar made that clear. Robinson was the first Negro—Rabin knew how to say the word properly, emphasizing the vowels in the first syllable as if the word contained three or four e's—to play professional baseball. It was not so long ago that Jews were kept from doing things too, not so much baseball, but other things, so we had to cheer for Jackie Robinson because it was almost the same as cheering for ourselves.

Rabin would have liked Robinson anyway. He liked his color, his black skin, though that was not the sort of thing you could say out loud to anyone. He liked the way Robinson was so fast on the base paths, so graceful pivoting on the double play, so good at the plate, and he never lost his temper, never yelled at other players, never argued with the umpire. This was more than you could say for Rabin's famous cousin, Happy Kasnoff, who during the early summer of '43 suddenly advanced from sandlot ball to the Royals because so many of the real players were serving their country overseas. Happy did not earn his nickname that season. When he lost a fly ball in the sun and it dropped three feet in front of him, and he fumbled picking it up and then threw it into the infield too late to prevent two runs from scoring, Happy slammed his mitt to the ground. Once when he was called out on strikes, he turned around and said something Rabin couldn't understand, and then Happy, the catcher, and the umpire were in a tight group, shoving each other back and forth. A couple of minutes later, Happy was on his way to the showers.

Jackie Robinson never did anything embarrassing like that. He was *a credit to his race.* Everyone said that. At Willingdon School in the Opportunity Class, made up of twenty third-graders picked from all over Montreal, they said the same thing about Paul Smith. Almost the same color as Jackie Robinson, Paul was shy and rarely talked to his classmates, and on the playground he was not even as good a ballplayer as Rabin. Once in class when Miss Briggs asked who could name a large body of water off the West Coast of North America, both Paul's and Rabin's hands shot into the air. Certain that his had been up first, Rabin felt it was unfair when Miss Briggs looked at him and then called on Paul. *The Potomac,* said the Black youngster, and Rabin felt himself blushing. *Sorry, but that's not correct,* said Miss Briggs. *The Potomac is a large river, but it's on the*

East Coast. *It flows through the American capital, Washington, D.C., where President Truman lives.* She turned to Rabin. He said *the Pacific Ocean* and shrank back. Paul Smith should have known that; if he had, Rabin would not have felt this strange sense of shame that made it difficult for him to look at his classmate for the next week.

After Poughkeepsie they did not stop, but raced along the Henry Hudson Parkway toward Manhattan as the speedometer needle kept pointing farther and farther to the right.

Not so fast, Hannah kept saying. *You've got plenty of time.*

You call this fast? Lazar pushed his foot down to the floor. *C'mon. We used to drive to New York in six hours; we used to leave Montreal at midnight and get into Manhattan for an early breakfast. Remember?*

Yes I remember—LAZAR, NOT SO FAST!—that was a long time ago.

At the two-room suite in the Astor Hotel, Hannah closed the blinds, took two aspirin, and got in bed.

You take him to lunch. It's an hour until you have to meet Harry Friedman.

Uncle Harry's here?

Aren't you hungry? said Lazar, moving him out the door and into the hot streets. Rabin was always hungry. The sun was blazing. The delicatessen on Broadway was hot and steamy, jammed with men in shirtsleeves, their ties pulled away from their necks, their collar buttons open. Rabin had been hoping for a fancy restaurant, a real New York fancy restaurant like the kind they usually went to.

Dad, I don't like this place. Let's go somewhere else.

Don't be silly. This is a great deli.

I don't want to eat in a deli. I want to go to a nice restaurant. This place is dirty. It's too hot.

Listen, Rabin. This is the deli where I became famous last year. Remember?

Yeah, I remember. Rabin did not speak so much as groan. He had heard the story at least a million times. Lazar continued as if the events had taken place just yesterday.

It was April of '45, just a couple of days after FDR died and almost nobody knew what Harry Truman looked like. I came here for lunch and someone said out loud, That's him, that's Harry, *and people began to point and the owner rushed up to me and said* Mr., er, President. I'm so honored you come to my place for lunch, *and before I could answer he began shouting at busboys and waiters to clear away some tables for the President. And people were getting up, and someone went to the phone to call the press, and some people kind of bowed toward me and others waved and yelled* Harry, you give it to those goddamn Japs. . . .

Lazar was gazing around the scene of his greatest triumph with a great big smile on his face. *Do you want to know what happened when they found out?*

S'pose, mumbled Rabin.

Well, we all had a great big laugh. And the owner—he gave me a free lunch anyway.

The table was ready now. Rabin's frankfurters and beans were the best he had ever eaten, the best—he would know forty years later—that he ever would eat. Lazar rushed him to finish, rushed him back to the hotel, and rushed off to his appointment. The big room was dark and Hannah was still asleep. Rabin sat in his own room reading the latest Hardy Boys adventure, but this was New York. You didn't come to New York to read, and when would he get here again? He stood by Hannah's bed.

Mom, I'm bored.

She groaned.

Can't we go to a show? Let's go to a show. There's lots of them right near the hotel.

Another groan. One minute later Rabin went down on an elevator all alone with the operator, an old man the color of Jackie Robinson who wore a splendid maroon suit with a double row of big shining brass buttons. At the ground floor he said, *Watch your step, son.* The lobby was wonderful—everything was big, glittery, polished, and new, and all the people hurrying by, or sitting in the soft red sofas, looked serious and rich. Outside the streets were crowded. Broadway was so much wider than any street in Montreal, and Times Square—not really a square, anyone could see that—was crowded with all kinds of people, and a bunch of movie theaters with blazing marquees, and thousands of cars and buses roaring along, and words flashing news in lights up on the triangular Times building, and billboards all over the tops of buildings around the square. The best one was for Camel Cigarettes, the face of a man blowing smoke rings every few seconds, big smoke rings maybe ten feet across, each one perfectly circular when it left the hole in the sign between his painted lips, the circle slowly distending and deforming and wisping away as it sailed across the square.

In front of the Newsreel Theater, Rabin was stopped by the phrase in big letters: *The Face of the Death Camps—THE GREATEST HUMAN HORROR EVER SEEN.* Uncle Ziggy and other relatives he had only heard about had been in such camps, but the photos on display startled him. Could these really be people, their bodies bony and stacked into piles like cordwood or heaped into mounds in ditches watched over by American soldiers with rifles on their shoulders. Some of the skeletons were alive, staring directly at Rabin with burning eyes that made him turn away. But something pulled him back again. Could this be Uncle Ziggy, or somebody else's uncle, looking up from the stretcher that was being loaded into a Red Cross truck, his eyes burning out of the picture with questions. What did he want from Rabin?

There you are, shouted Lazar. He grabbed Rabin and hugged him. *We've been looking all over for you.* Harry Friedman stood next to Lazar. *We thought you'd gotten lost.*

Uncle Harry, are you coming to California too?

No, champ. Lazar put Rabin down. *Someone's got to make sure everything stays OK back in Montreal now that the Rotensteins are leaving.*

Rabin liked Harry Friedman, who was not really an uncle, but their neighbor across the street—at least he had been when they had a house on Vendome. Harry was always full of smiles. He had a tiny, round wife named Budgie, who wore lots of makeup and very high heels and came, so Hannah said, directly from *the chorus line— where she belonged,* and a daughter, Bubbles, Rabin's age, who wore shiny dresses that looked too old for her, and three dogs, a slow-witted Great Dane named Duke and two yappy Mexican hairless named

Tic and Toc. That was also the name of Harry's night club, at least the most recent one. Harry always owned a night club. A couple of years ago it had been the El Morocco, but they were all much the same. For Rabin's tenth birthday just a few months before, they had all gone to the dinner show at the Tic Toc. Lazar and Hannah, Chaim Baer and David, Moishe, Ida and Sheila—they all sat at a table right on the edge of the dance floor. Rabin was so excited that he could not stop eating, even during the acts—the chorus girls and dancers, the jugglers, and the comedian. A young singer named Dean Martin seemed bothered by Rabin's chewing. *This kid,* he waved the spotlight onto Rabin, *hasn't stopped eating for a moment. He must think it's the Last Supper!* Rabin turned beet red in all the laughter. After the show, Harry brought the singer over to meet the birthday boy: *No hard feelings, huh, kid? In this business you do anything for a laugh.*

Hannah liked Harry too. Back at the hotel room, the shades were up.

Bridget, said Harry. *You're as beautiful as ever. You're leaving behind a lot of broken hearts in Montreal. Including mine.*

Did Hannah blush? *I'll bet you say that to all the girls.*

Lazar produced a bottle of Johnny Walker, and soon the adults were all ignoring Rabin and laughing a lot and saying *Remember when* this and *Remember when* that and then talking about a lot of things that made no sense to Rabin and laughing some more. The laughter continued even after Uncle Elliot arrived. He was a real uncle, Hannah's brother. Together they all went up to the roof of the Astor. Harry left before they ordered dinner.

I wonder what her name is, said Hannah.

Uncle Elliot raised his glass: *To family. To safe traveling. To success in California. To becoming Americans.*

We are already *Americans.* Rabin felt annoyed. *Canada's just as much part of America as the United States.*

Elliot smiled: *Here we call ourselves Americans and the people north of the border Canadians.*

Well, it's not fair. You can look on a map and see.

Who knows if we'll become Americans? said Hannah.

Just wait till you pick oranges right off your own tree for breakfast, said Lazar. *Just wait till you see the palm trees and the beaches.*

Look at me. I was just as scared when I came here. America has been good to me. Soon you'll love America.

The United States, said Rabin.

After the excitement of the Holland Tunnel under the Hudson River the next morning, New Jersey was boring. Even before they entered the tunnel with a mass of cars and trucks, Rabin began to worry, *What if it begins to leak? What if the water rushes in and we're all drowned?* All through the long minutes underwater, as they drove slowly, too slowly—*Why is the speed limit 45?*—through the sickly yellow light reflected off the shiny tiles, he was so nervous he forgot to ask Lazar to blow his horn, and Lazar forgot to offer. A few hours later Rabin was wishing for another tunnel to liven things up. New Jersey was at first all factories and dumps, a wasteland of dark buildings with broken windows, heaps of rusted cars and old machinery, mounds of indescribable junk, and awful smells that made Lazar close the windows. Then it became green and flat, flat as a pancake and completely boring.

Boring as a synagogue on Yom Kippur.

Lazar laughed. Hannah turned around and stared. Rabin began to bounce up and down.

Boring as Sunday school. Boring as a Hebrew lesson. Boring as a Seder.

That's enough, said Hannah.

He's right, said Lazar. *Seders are really boring.*

I wish you wouldn't encourage him.

I don't need encouragement to think religion is boring, Mom. It's boring. Boring as New Jersey.

The feeling that began that afternoon would last for eleven days, long days of confinement in the car, days broken only by brief stops in gas stations and restaurants, days made longer by the fact that in his rush to get to California, Lazar insisted on driving eight, ten, twelve hours a day. Combating the boredom was not easy. You could sing *Freres Jacques* or *Row, Row, Row Your Boat* only so many times, play Twenty Questions and Hangman just so much, spend just so many hours looking for license plates from different states. The first one from California—black figures on an orange background—was a thrill, but after they had noted plates from only twenty-five states, Rabin grew tired of looking. He slumped in the backseat, staring at the countryside. So many hours with *nothing to do* gave him lots of time to think about where he was and where he was going.

They were entering unknown territory. Upstate New York and Manhattan were places they took vacations, had relatives, visited regularly. But New Jersey was new to him, and farther on the land would be even more unfamiliar: Pennsylvania, Indiana, Illinois—names out of history and geography books, places with cities that baseball teams came from—the Phillies, the Pirates, the White Sox, the Cubs. Each state they crossed would mean that Montreal was farther away. Harry Friedman would not call him *champ* tonight, nor Uncle Elliot toast them. From here on it was strangers all the way. In California the only people they knew were relatives—Lazar's sister Polly, her daughter Clara and her husband, Willy, and their son Bobby, who had won a quick reputation when he had visited Montreal last year. Even Cousin Morty couldn't keep up with Bobby. Together the two stole magazines and soft drinks from candy stores on the Main, sprinting away from outraged storekeepers and once outrunning a cop, tearing down streets and alleys, jumping over fences, crashing through backyards. Bobby ripped holes in three pairs of good pants in two weeks and had a punch-out with a *brute* of a guy (Bobby's description) who did not like the idea of a fourteen-year-old barging through his rosebushes. Bobby's shiner was the envy of all his cousins. Sheila kept wanting to touch it, but Bobby pushed her away. *Rabin,* he said. *When you come to California, I'll show you how to have a* really *good time!*

Were all the kids in California like Bobby? The idea worried me. Cousin Morty was rough enough, and all he did was cut school to drink beer and go to burlesque houses. Rabin's friends who lived on Vendome did not steal or drink beer or cut school. They played softball and they all got pretty good grades and they all knew what they would be when they grew up. Mitchell Klein was going to become an accountant like his dad, and Arthur Stampleman a dentist like his. Jerry Held would take over his father's pharmacy on Sherbrooke. Melvin Schwartz, whose sister, Joy, had the biggest breasts of all the girls not only on Vendome but in all of Montreal (or so cousin Morty said)—Melvin, when he stopped selling tickets for people to peer through a hole in the wall from his bedroom into his sister's when she was undressing—of course, she knew they were watching, and Jerry, who lived next door, even said she shared the profits with Morty, fifty-fifty—why, Melvin would no doubt collect junk just like his father.

It wasn't a great occupation—not even after Melvin's father, during the war, began to call himself a Scrap Metal Dealer and got a B gas ration sticker for his car. But at least it was an occupation. Lazar, unlike other fathers, did not seem to have an occupation, or a profession, or even a job. He did occasionally own a business. Too many businesses—Freehold Finance, General Metal, Beaumaire Plastering, Acme Construction, Millen Freres Lumber—and each for only a short period of time. And no matter which one he owned, Lazar did not really work very much. At least he was never gone from home for very long. Every morning he would drive Rabin to Willingdon School. He wanted to pick him up in the afternoon too, but Rabin found it so embarrassing to have his father in the car, waiting for a hello kiss, that he preferred to take the bus home instead. Lazar was almost always there when he arrived, ready to help get cookies and milk for his son.

Both of Rabin's brothers had their futures set. Chaim Baer was going to be a pianist or a composer like Uncle Elliot, and after graduating from the University of Lower California, David would be in business administration, whatever that was. Lazar and Hannah seemed to approve of these choices, but they were less happy with the only professional desire Rabin ever expressed. Two years before, after seeing the Ballets Russe de Monte Carlo three times in two weeks (once on a field trip with the Opportunity Class, once with Hannah, and once again, after he begged and begged, with cousin Lionel's wife, Cora), Rabin began to leap about the living room and say that he wanted to be a dancer just like Anton Dolin. Chaim Baer teased him unmercifully: *You're so fat you'd break the floor of the au-*

ditorium. David told the guys on the block, who came at Rabin in a whirl of fists and kicking feet that left him more scared than bruised, though his nose was a touch bloody. *Fairy, fairy,* they kept yelling. *They meant the Nutcracker,* said Hannah, who seemed to have something wrong with her eye. Lazar tried to look stern, but he kept smiling: *Better forget about ballet. Seems dangerous.* Hannah agreed: *Its probably not a good idea.*

· · · ═══════

Years later, the chief images from the trip that would stay with Rabin would be those of his father, hurrying, always hurrying into the car, through meals, out of restrooms. Wanting to drive faster and farther each day. Always in a rush, always getting excited, always breaking into a *temper.* Becoming angry at something or someone for slowing them down. Waiters, gas station attendants, hotel clerks—nobody moved fast enough to suit Lazar. On the Pennsylvania Turnpike it was the counter girl at Howard Johnson's who brought fried clams instead of french fries. *Try them,* insisted Lazar. *They're just as good as potatoes, and we don't have time to send them back.* Rabin made a face and pushed them away. Lazar picked one up, popped it into his mouth, and began to chew. A moment later he was gagging and spitting into his napkin. *They're not kosher,* said Hannah. Late Sunday afternoon in St. Louis, the outdoor temperature of 106 degrees was cool compared to the steamy, jammed restaurant where Lazar raged at a harassed-looking waiter, first for not bringing a second pitcher of ice water fast enough, then for the soggy, undercooked fried chicken: *Take this back and get it cooked.*

Cook it yourself, the waiter yelled back, refusing to come near the Rotenstein table again. Lazar turned purple and his forehead was bulging when Hannah stood up, took Rabin by the hand, and led him outdoors and to a nearby market. That night they ate baloney, lettuce, and tomato sandwiches sitting on the porch of a yellow tile motel and listened to local announcers lament Rudy York's tenth-inning homer that gave the Red Sox a victory over the Cards in the opening game of the Series.

More than one of the delays were brought on by Lazar's own impatience. Somewhere in Illinois he drove right past a detour sign and slammed into a pile of gravel, to the cheers of a bunch of highway workmen sitting on the beds of trucks, munching sandwiches. On the rolling highway outside Tucumcari, he shrugged off the dark mountains of threatening clouds pointed out by a nervous Hannah and gestured impatiently at the repeated signs warning of flash floods: *That's for people who don't know how to drive.* The clouds opened wide when the Packard was at the top of a hill; the rushing water struck it at the bottom, skimming the car like a stone on a river and spinning it into a ditch. While they waited for the tow truck, Lazar blamed the tires: *Retreads. These aren't new tires. That goniff Sheinbaum sold me retreads!*

It was the second time those tires let him down. Five days earlier, they took a room in an Indianapolis motor court where all the lamps had twenty-watt bulbs, and—nagged by the bored ten-year-old Rabin—went off on a moonless night to a movie in a rundown section of town where the streetlights were not working. After the show, the right front tire of the car was flat. Lazar struggled with the jack for a while, and just when he and Hannah began to exchange sharp words, two Black men emerged from the darkness. After a long, speechless moment, they offered to help. While they changed the wheel, Lazar hovered over them, gesturing vaguely. When they finished, he tipped each man a dollar. They smiled, touched fingers to the narrow brims of their hats, and vanished. On the way back to the motel, Lazar was pulled over by a cop for speeding through a residential area.

The Packard itself was the cause of more than one delay. Somewhere beyond Vinita the generator light came on and stayed on, forcing a midafternoon stop in Oklahoma City. At the Packard agency Lazar slipped ten dollars to the head mechanic, only to be told the shop couldn't possibly get to his car until the next day. Another ten moved the time up to later that same afternoon, when it turned out that there was nothing wrong with the generator; all the car needed was a new fuse. Three days later, just past Boulder Dam, the light came on again. A Las Vegas mechanic in a dusty gas station shook his head in wonder: *Can't understand how you got so far with such a bum generator. It ain't chargin' nothin'. It's a miracle your bat-tery's not dead.*

Could he fix it? Sure, but it would take three days for the parts to arrive from Los Angeles. Lazar couldn't wait that long. A quick charge of the battery and then he would be on his way. The mechanic scratched his head in wonder.

You're a brave man, he said. *Bad enough with that bum generator. You'd be downright crazy to try the desert without a water bag.*

A water bag? said Lazar.

Yeah. Lots of radiators boil over on the way to L.A. You could re-ally use two of them. Just to be sure.

One's enough, said Lazar, forking over five dollars. The mecha-nic hung the brown canvas bag, bulging with water, over the front bumper.

Dad, it's dripping, said Rabin. *Should it leak like that?*

Kids, said the mechanic. *Know it all. Sonny, they're supposed to leak like that. Keeps the water cool.*

Rabin, they're supposed to leak like that, said his father.

Outside Las Vegas, Rabin kept his eyes glued to the thermometer. The needle edged slowly to the right. *It's getting hot, Dad,* he kept saying. *Naah. It's at 180, just where it's supposed to be,* was the re-sponse until, on the long grade outside Yermo, the needle suddenly zoomed all the way into the red zone. Lazar stopped the car, smiling one of his rare smiles, a smile that lasted until he reached the front of the car and found the water bag, still hanging on the bumper, but now limp, empty, and only slightly damp. Before help could reach them, Hannah had fainted from the heat.

The need to rush meant that Lazar was rarely prepared to stop for the purpose of sight-seeing. In the East and Midwest, he passed up haunted houses, banks that had been robbed by famous criminals, hotels where presidents slept, and local museums, saying, *We'll stop later. Out West there's better sights.* But Out West it wasn't much dif-ferent. He refused to turn off for Carlsbad Caverns or Meteor Crater because they were *too far off the road.* Somewhere in Arizona, loudly announcing that it was not true he never stopped for sights, Lazar did pull off the highway at the Petrified Forest, which was directly on

Highway 66. For a few minutes the three of them stared at a bleak, empty area of scrub brush studded with small, dark outcroppings. *Dad, are those the petrified trees? Why do they look like rocks? How am I supposed to know? I'm not a geologist!*

Later that day, Lazar agreed to drive a few extra miles to the Painted Desert in search of a *bargain* hotel that proved to have plenty of rooms but no heating. They went on to Flagstaff and stayed in a neat, knotty-pine motel with a Franklin stove and a roof that leaked during the night's thunderstorms. At the South Rim of the Grand Canyon the next day, Lazar began to look at his watch after ten minutes. When Rabin began to talk about riding a mule down to the Colorado River, his father dragged him back to the car.

Rabin was not silent about his disappointment over the lack of sight-seeing. To him, it fit into a pattern: Chaim Baer and David got to go everywhere—Florida, Atlantic City, Niagara Falls—while his parents never took him anywhere.

That's not true, said Hannah. *We didn't take your brothers to Cuba, and they were plenty jealous that you went with us.*

Were they? He had been so young—four or five—that he could hardly remember anything beyond the awful taste of the fried eggs on the ship and his mother saying: *Can't we get anything that's not cooked in olive oil?* After that he ate a lot of oatmeal and spent a lot of time at the back of the ship on the lower deck near a small cannon that was covered with canvas until a sailor in blue unwrapped it to show all the kids how it swiveled around and how you could aim it. Rabin stood in line to take a turn looking through the sighting mechanism, but he saw no more than a reflection of his own eyelashes. When someone asked, *What's it used for?* the sailor answered, *To keep away German subs.* After it was covered again, Rabin hung around, hoping a U-boat would appear.

All he remembered of Havana was the feeling of a sun so bright that it hurt his eyes, the surprising taste of fresh pineapple juice at street-corner stands, and the gentle-feeling, dark-faced presence of José, who took care of him when his parents were out. More vivid was the train ride back to New York, when he had a stomachache and threw up all night long. They arrived at Grand Central at six-thirty in the morning, too early for any doctors or pharmacies to be open, so to keep him quiet, his parents took Rabin to a movie, *Beware of Spooks,* which featured a lot of Negro men with huge white smiles who rolled their eyes and did a lot of funny things. Most hilarious was the part when, to get away from someone who was chasing them, the main characters ran up a staircase that, just before they got to the top, collapsed into a slide, and shrieking and thrashing they tumbled back to the ground. The same thing happened again and again, but no matter how many times they slid back, the men never stopped trying to escape up that trick staircase. Ever after, the sequence would stay with Rabin, the image of those scrambling Black men, almost at their goal when at the very last instant the staircase collapsed beneath them and all came tumbling down.

Cuba was a long time ago.

Five years is not so long, said Hannah.

Why did we go to Cuba?

His parents looked at each other.

Well, your Uncle Moishe and I owned part of a mine there. A tungsten mine on the Isle of Pines off the southern coast. It wasn't working properly, wasn't producing enough tungsten to make a profit. You know what tungsten is? The government needed it for the war. It's used to make the filaments in electric lights so that the lights can glow.

Oh.

We never did get it working. Lazar shook his head. *The machinery was old and rusty. The Germans who worked it were all in camps, and the Cubans didn't know how to run things.*

After we get to California, let's go back to Cuba, Dad. Let's go on the yacht.

Yacht? said Hannah. *What yacht?*

The one Daddy's going to buy to sail us down the coast to Honolulu.

Yeah, that one, said Lazar.

Honolulu is not on the coast. It's on an island. Hannah's voice did not sound very motherly, and nobody had anything to say back to her.

· · ═══ ═══

The Cuba story ought to have been a tip-off, but Rabin was only ten. Decades later it would finally occur to him that it was more than a little strange to think his father, who would hardly have known a mine from a mountain peak, let alone tungsten from coal, could have expected to oversee the restoration of such a facility. Reading about American financial interests in Cuba provided a better explanation: in the thirties, Meyer Lansky and a few of his friends wanted to turn the Isle of Pines into a major gambling resort. By this time Rabin believed that there was something special about coming from a family of racketeers, and he had begun to refer to his heritage as *Mafioso. Romanian Mafioso.*

Mafioso? The wife of a colleague or a donor, a woman with a pearl necklace in basic black, looks as if she fears something may be wrong with her hearing.

Like in the movies. Gangsters. You know: numbers, making book, rum running during prohibition—that sort of thing.

Oh is the reply, or *Indeed,* or *How interesting,* then she finds an excuse to turn away. To this, like all rules, there were exceptions: the stocky, handsome woman a decade Rabin's senior who stares him straight in the eye and says: *Do you carry a big gun too?* It's just possible that he blushes a touch before finding an excuse to turn away. She is, after all, the wife of a trustee.

Each of Lazar's children found out about their father's occupation in a different way. David learned at the age of sixteen in a train on the way back from Toronto, where he had attended a national meeting of the AZA, the B'nai Brith youth organization, and had lodged for three days with a Polish family that ate—he would never get over this until, thirty years later, his second wife would be a woman born in Kraków—soup for breakfast. A friend introduced him to a tough-looking kid from the East Side, who said with great enthusiasm, *David Rotenstein? Great. Your Dad's the Numbers King of Canada!* Chaim Baer found out just before his high school graduation when Lazar took him for an uncharacteristic Sunday ride in the country and, parked by a lake or a forest, or maybe sitting in front of a soda shop in a small town named after a French saint, confessed in an embarrassed voice that he was ashamed of his occupation: *Please, don't think less of me,* he said to a seventeen-year-old who for the first time felt proud of his father.

Life in California sheltered Rabin from the past—or was he a bit retarded?—for he did not learn until the age of nineteen, and he was almost as shocked as later academic listeners would be. It was during the early summer of 1955, on his first trip back to Montreal. He and Cousin Morty were sitting in the Snowden Deli—Ben's was closed and its owner living in Florida—eating smoked-meat sandwiches. Morty looked prosperous in a suit and tie, and it was difficult for Rabin, wearing his uniform of jeans and a work shirt, to believe that only three years separated them.

I'm out of Dad's racket, you know? No more horses and books; no more worries about runners with sticky fingers. The money's in the legal rackets now—construction, parking lots, government contracts.

Horses? Books? Rackets?

It's never been the same since your old man pulled out, you know that? Dad says its never been the same, and he should know. Lazar and Moishe: they were quite a team—the kingpins, that's what Dad says.

Morty, pausing to chew, looked uncharacteristically solemn.

Rabin, you guys shouldn't have gone. You and me—if you were still here, we could have been like Moishe and Lazar. Your dad broke up a great team. The whole family looked up to them when they were together, but Moishe on his own . . . it's never been the same.

A pause for chewing.

Your dad didn't just invent the payoff system. What he really did was keep Moishe honest, keep him human. You know, everyone really liked your dad—Charlie, Dudele, Hymie, my Dad, everyone, they all trusted him. And he pulled the plug on them; he pulled the plug on all of us.

That night Rabin asked Uncle Moishe for details. They were strolling just behind Sheila and Ida on the Main toward the bagel factory after a dinner at Moishe's. Rabin had hardly recognized the place: the narrow staircase well lit and covered with plush blue carpet; the tables with linen cloths and napkins, wine glasses rather than tumblers, bright silverware, flowers in tiny vases; and instead of Moishe in a white apron, they were greeted by a head waiter with a slight French accent wearing a tux. A tux! The steak was not as good as in memory, but the chopped liver and onions provided a pleasantly familiar feeling of heartburn.

Tell me about the old days, said Rabin.

What about them?

Bookmaking. Rabin paused. *Numbers.*

Who have *you been talking to?*

No one in particular.

Morty, said Moishe. *Why don't you ask your father?*

He's in California.

Morty! Sometimes he talks about Israel. Sometimes he talks about the good old days. I wish he'd make up his mind. What's the matter with him?

Did you and Dad start here on the Main?

Who can remember?

C'mon.

It was a long time ago. We were young, we had to make a living. What did we know? We knew from nothing. It was a long time ago.

Two months later in California, Lazar said: *It was a business. We ran it like any other business. Sure we paid off the cops—that was one of our regular expenses. Everything else was legit. The betting was strictly on the up and up. We paid off our winners like clockwork. During the war I took home five thousand a week, no taxes.*

How come you never told me?

What good would it do you? It would help you at school? We left Montreal to get you away from all that.

There was something else that Lazar never told Rabin, something that helped to explain why his normally impatient father was on the edge of hysteria during that twelve-day journey in 1946, something that helped to explain the rushing, the jumpiness, the anger, the desire to stay in hotels in the center of towns rather than motels out on lonely roads. The words were voiced by Hannah when Lazar was in the hospital.

Two hundred fifty thousand dollars? Rabin was stunned as his mind fled backward thirty years.

That's why we had to stop in New York. Canadians weren't allowed to take money out of the country. Harry Friedman got it for him. He gave that much to Harry in Montreal, and Harry got him the same amount in New York.

In cash? said Rabin. *How'd you carry it?*

Money belts. We each had wads of bills in belts around our waist. Didn't you notice how fat I looked? I wasn't so fat, not then. We all get fat sooner or later.

Not Rabin. He got thinner as he got older, just like his father. His memory improved too. At the age of twenty-five he could hardly remember the 1946 trip across the country; in his fifties, the incidents of the journey grew clearer and clearer in his mind. Of all the nights of that trip, the one he remembered most clearly was the fourth, the night after a drive across Pennsylvania on the new turnpike, which advertised itself as the most beautiful highway in the world. Late in the afternoon they reached Wheeling, West Virginia. It looked like a toy city, jammed as it was into a green valley with a river, arched bridges, brick houses on the hillsides, the smokestacks of factories, a few tall buildings, one of them with a large clock tower. At the best hotel, they learned that a convention was on. *We only have one room left, it's the last room in town,* said the manager. *I'm afraid it's not our best.*

Let's look at it, said Hannah.

They went up in an elevator that smelled of alcohol with a bellhop and half a dozen men in brown suits, their faces red. The room was on the top floor, with bright yellow wallpaper, a slanting roof, and no window.

How can you rent a room with no window, Lazar yelled at the manager across the front desk, while Hannah sharply whispered, *Shaa, Lazar.* Rabin had wandered away to look longingly in the cigar and candy counter across the lobby. Thirty years later he would stay in a room without a window, a much smaller room in Nagoya, Japan, a room wholly filled by a double bed. When the air conditioning went off in the middle of the night, he woke with a start, feeling as if he had been buried alive. There proved to be no way to keep the heavy metal door from swinging shut, so he had stuck a shoe between it and the jambs to let in air so that he could get a few hours sleep. The shoe was so twisted from the weight of the door that he could never wear it comfortably again.

It's clean, isn't it? said the manager.

IT DOESN'T HAVE A WINDOW! Lazar's eyes were bulging and a vein stood out on his forehead. Hannah took his arm and began to pull him away.

Jews, said the manager to nobody in particular as he turned his back.

A few miles before reaching Wheeling, they had seen some nice white cabins in a steep green valley along a rushing stream. A bit rustic but clean and tranquil. You could hear the sweet rush of water, the last sounds of birds in the great willows bending against the twilight, the occasional hum of a car on the highway. Beginning at midnight you could also hear the freight trains roaring so close behind the cabin that the first had all three of them sitting upright in bed, the lights on, staring at each other in stark terror. Lazar rushed over, picked up Rabin and began to herd Hannah toward the door as the sound of the train grew louder and louder and it seemed that in a moment it would suddenly burst right through the walls of the cabin and grind them to death.

After midnight the trains ran every half hour. Each time it was a little less frightening, and eventually Hannah and Rabin fell into fitful sleeps. In the morning, Lazar, who *didn't sleep a wink,* was in a foul humor. They stood in front of the cabin, gazing at a line of trees that hid the railroad tracks. The air was cool and fresh, the sun touching the trees high up in the canyon, the river peaceful. The trains had stopped at dawn.

Didn't you see them? Lazar's voice was an accusation.

I liked the hotel, said Hannah.

Yeah, you're the one who wanted a window, Dad. If there was no window, we couldn't hear the trains.

Get in the car, said Lazar. *We've got a long way to go.*

The fashionable Hannah and Lazar during better days, shortly after their first child, Chaim Baer, was born. (He is in the buggy hidden in shadow at the back.)

EIGHT

Hannah's Lament

January 1, 1947. Wed. Today I saw the tournament of Roses parade. It had some very beautiful floats. In the Rosebowl football game UCLA lost to Illinois 45 to 14. Little Al Hoish made a 103-yard run to score UCLA's second touchdown. It was the longest run ever made in the Rose Bowl.

January 2, 1947. Thurs. Today was the first time I went back to school since the holidays which ended yesterday. There wasn't much work. In the afternoon I had a haircut. I also made a run in kickball, and three hits. Later in the afternoon I played a little football.

January 3, 1947. Fri. Today we had fun in arithmetic at school measuring on scale maps. We played football at recess and at noon. In the afternoon we played football. In the evening I went to a show with Daddy, Mommy, and cousin Clara. It was called "The Verdict." It was with Sidney Greenstreet, Peter Lorre, and Joan Lorring.

January 5, 1947. Sun. Today we had a big game of guns in the morning. Later on we had a football game. In the afternoon Herbie drove me up to Bobby's house and I went to a show with Bobby and Ronnie. The show was called "Pride of the Yankees" the life story of Lou Gehrig who was played by Gary Cooper.

January 6, 1947. Mon. Today we started a football league with two teams. Donald and Max are UCLA while Marshall and I are Illinois. Today we won 40 to 36.

January 7, 1947. Tues. Today in phys. ed. I got 14 baskets in one minute free throws for goal. I only had to get 12. In our football league it was a tie score 12 to 12.

January 8, 1947. Wed. Today in school I and three other boys were cutting cord for the pupils of the school to tie there scrap paper with because on this coming Friday we're having a scrap paper drive. In the afternoon we couldn't play any football with Marshall so the teams were Max and I against Donald and Stanley. We won 24 to 6.

January 9, 1947. Thu. Today we had fun in school in the afternoon. We went into Miss Wallaces room and saw a soundless movie called "Frontier Woman." In the football league the teams were Pete Patman and I against Max and Donald they won 18 to 12.

January 11, 1947. Sat. Today in the afternoon I went to the Hitching Post. I saw "Texas Masquerade" and "Stagecoach to Monterey." With it there was a serial, called "The Scarlet Rider." There was also a Bugs Bunny picture. Later on after the show I beat up Donald. We started boxing and he started slapping and hacking so I started wrestling. I grabbed him by his neck and I had him on his knees.

FROM THE DIARY OF RABIN ROTENSTEIN

Twenty-three years after her wedding, Hannah, in the Packard with Lazar and Rabin and on the way to California, silently disagreed with their notion that the Pennsylvania Turnpike was *beautiful.* How could a highway be beautiful? Paintings were beautiful, symphonies were beautiful, novels and poems were beautiful, waterfalls were beautiful. Highways were just a way of going from one place to another. Beautiful things were not used; they were things you simply enjoyed. They made you feel better about the world and about yourself, gave you something to live for when all else failed. As it usually did. Imagine Ida turning to her at dinner the night before they left Montreal and saying, *You think you can find more people in California who prefer Chopin to poker?*

That Ida, always ready with a dig—more than twenty years of digs. As if the move had been Hannah's idea. As if she hadn't cried and fought with Lazar about it for eight years. As if she had not thought of staying behind. As if she had not been glad when the authorities told him the Romanian quota would be filled for more than two decades and dismayed when Al Altdorfer—he of the goyische *wife, a real beauty to be sure—who had moved to Hartford so nobody would remember on which side of the Main he had been born or what his mother's profession had been (if you can call that a profession)—sure Al would have been more than happy to get Lazar and his family into the United States, especially if there was a buck, or quite a few bucks, to be made out of the transaction. How much did this move cost Lazar? Never had he told her; never would he tell her, but it was certainly in the tens of thousands. And all to go somewhere where they didn't know a soul except for Polly and her daughter, Clara, who is little better than, you should pardon the expression, a* you-know-what, *and her two-bit bookie husband, Willy, hardly an improvement over Duke Hall, Bobby's father, except in height. Imagine marrying a man whose claim to fame is running those* meshuggane Marathon Dances. *Compared to that crooked racket, numbers looks pretty good. At least nobody gets cheated; that's what Papa told me. Hall sure was a looker. He sure looked me up and down that time we first met in New York, and I loved the way he said* How can Clara's aunt be as young as Clara? Bobby has his father's looks, but he'll come to the same sort of end—just disappear and never be heard of again. *The Mob. At least Moishe and Lazar got out when the getting was good—I'll give them that. Not that Hector Robaire wasn't a looker, and he looked at me that way too, more than once, but he gave me the willies. You could always see the holster and the gun bulging under his jacket.*

Men. You live with a man for twenty years, and you still don't know him. And he doesn't know you. Doesn't have an inkling. Lazar never notices the way Harry Friedman looks at me, never noticed the way Duke Hall looked at me, or the way Hector Robaire would make little complimentary remarks in French, which made his words sexier: I admit that. Otherwise how could he send me off with him alone in a snowmobile to pick up Rabin at the station in St. Agathe?

So close and warm in there and the window frosted and steamed so that nobody could see in. Didn't he stop by the side of the road and didn't he move over and put his arm around me and call me cheri *and say a bunch of words that I didn't exactly understand but that didn't keep me from knowing what he wanted and what—God, how can I admit it even to myself?—I for an instant wanted too. One kiss, one long kiss and me kissing back, but it wasn't really like Julius—I didn't even know that's what I expected—and when he put his hand on my breast it wasn't so difficult to sit up straight and say,* My son is waiting at the station, Hector, *and to push him away. He brought his face close again.* Hector, enough is enough. I'm a married woman.

Another time, cheri, *when there is more time,* he said and I didn't answer. I really didn't know what to say.

Lazar always knows what to say, even when he doesn't know what he's talking about. Moishe's the same—it's a trait that runs in the family. Chaim Baer and David have it already, and Rabin, my baby, seems to be developing it. Rotenstein men. My babies and they become Rotenstein men. Men who know it all even when they don't know a damn thing—such as how a woman wants to be touched, such as how a mother feels. Stubborn as can be too, and Lazar the most stubborn of all. Nobody, but nobody, thought this move was a good one. It wasn't just me or Mama and Papa. His brothers and his sisters all said the same thing: For God's sake, don't be crazy. What's in California but a bunch of fruits and nuts? What do you know from California? In California they'll eat you like cherries and spit out the pits. *And what does he answer, Mr. Know-it-all:* Montreal's small time. I've got bigger fish to fry.

As if he could fry a fish any more than he could catch one. What a laugh. All the tackle he bought, the fancy flannel shirts, the rods, the flies, the sport hats, the rubber boots. We Rotenstein men are going fishing, *he announces, and the three of them—thank God I kept Rabin home with me—disappear into the woods for a week. Do they bring home fish? I should live so long. It rains, the boat capsizes, Chaim Baer almost drowns, David gets his famous croup, and Lazar sprains his wrist from casting the wrong way with his rod. They all come home exhausted and sick and Lazar is in a foul humor (as*

usual) and the fishing stuff gets stuck away in a corner of the base-
ment. If I'm lucky there will be no fish in California—but there's sure
to be something else he can be absolutely impossible about.
Like this trip. Who else would drive all the way to California?
Other people sell their cars and take a nice train with a nice com-
partment, and when they get to California they buy another car. You
can't get a car like this today, *he says.* A 1940 Packard with only
37,000 miles. It's almost new. They're not building cars like this anymore. *Maybe not, but they are building some kinds of cars again, and*
anything would be better than this trip. How many hills and cows
and fields and billboards can you look at before you go stark raving
mad? No wonder I have a headache all the time. Him and his cars.
The Cord, the Pierce-Arrow, the Stutz. Always something new, some-
thing fancier. The latest design, the latest engine, the latest, widest
whitewall tires. Thank goodness for small blessings; at least this one is
comfortable and roomy, or it would be if we didn't have all of Rabin's
sports stuff and games jammed into the backseat—Batter Up and
First Down and Monopoly, two mitts and a bat, and a hockey stick.
Who, pray tell, plays hockey in California? Why couldn't we ship all
his stuff? No one's going to play with it on the trip.

I wish Lazar didn't encourage him, indulge his every desire. But
I should be honest. I do the same thing. How can I not? If anything
happened to him, I couldn't go on living. Not after Baby Seymour.
Yes, it was my fault for leaving him with the maid while talking to
Lillian Portigal for so long, and about what? Her problems with her
husband, Max. Eight years married and he's ignoring her or having
trouble in bed, and she thinks that maybe something is going on with
his new secretary. She should be so lucky, that's why he's so tired. And
I'm making soothing sounds because I know it isn't easy for her to
talk about these things (or for me to listen), and I'm thinking: things
could be worse. Who needs that male brutality anyway; I could have
done with a lot less of Lazar—except for the result, the babies. And in
comes the stupid girl, right into the bedroom without knocking, and
she sort of wails, M'dame, come queeck. Zee babee...

God punished me, I know that. But what for? You can't watch
them every minute of the day, can you? Or was it for my thoughts?

You have to do it with your husband, but does it say anywhere you have to like it? Is that in the Bible? The Talmud? Mama never liked it with Papa, I know that. Lena is lucky. Paul's too weak or sick most of the time, but that doesn't stop her from complaining. But she knew. He told her when he proposed. But to know is one thing, to live another. She was lucky; after all, she was no spring chicken, well over thirty, and he is a nice man. Treats her with respect. Doesn't roar around like Romanians. Romanians! Sometimes I wish I'd never heard of them. Mama tried to tell me, but I wouldn't listen. Eighteen and knew it all. But that wasn't really it. It was Julius. My true love. I could have phoned him in New York when Lazar was getting the money and Bobby was off somewhere, but it would only make me cry again. Like after the time Lazar and I visited Julius in his offices, twenty-fifth floor on Madison Avenue, mind you, and he's never married. Still waiting for you—that's what his eyes said. Hannah, you didn't trust me; you didn't wait. Another punishment, but for what? I was a kid. I was scared. How could I give myself to him? What did I know?

Mama knew about Romanians, knew about Lazar despite the good front he always put on—flowers for her, candies for me, always dressed so fine, always smelling of good cologne, but Mama knew as soon as she met his mother. What an old wretch! But I didn't see that until months after the wedding when after one of her heavy dinners, and my stomach was aching as usual, she says right out loud that Lazar did not want to marry me but she forced him to because we both knew why. She even smiled a kind of horrible smile. Lazar said nothing but a weak Mama, and I wanted to sink through the floor. Imagine her saying right out that he had deflowered me before the wedding. Me! I had guarded myself not so much against Lazar—he had never tried to do more than kiss me and put his tongue in my mouth—but against Julius, my love, who had wanted me so badly for two years, especially in those months before he went off to Paris, when he was so unsure of himself, of the future, afraid, alone with an ailing mother, his breath always smelling of turnips and garlic. Would he have taken me with him if I had given in? No—that was just a fantasy. Julius was a man. He might be needy but his mind was made up. He loved me but for him love could not be the issue. Escaping poverty was the issue, and medical school was the way to do that, medical school in Paris because McGill did not care to turn out Jewish doctors unless they were young men from families who were able to add significantly to the school's endowment.

I can still hear Lazar's voice saying Mama so weakly, and see the old woman give him a look, the same look he always gives me when he's angry, a look that scared me then and scares me still, and he doesn't let out another peep all the time she goes on making me feel like two cents and suddenly I realize that I am married to a miserable cur. Me, crazy Hannah they called me, and eight months after getting married I'm already the most unhappy girl in the world. And what does Mama do? Slaps my face and says, You wanted to get married, you're married. You expected a bed of roses? You think your father with his silences—sometimes I don't hear his voice for days, not talking to me, not directly, not saying anything I want to hear—and his movies is such a perpetual barrel of monkeys? At least Lazar makes a good living, *kaina hora,* while me, I've got to live with a boarder all my life. You think that's such a pleasure? Just for once it would be nice to have a whole refrigerator and not give up a shelf for someone else or go to my own bathroom and not have to deal with someone else's soap and towels or to be able to sit for as long as I like and not worry that someone else needs to use it. It would even be nice to sleep in a room with some real privacy and not be separated from a stranger by no more than a set of French doors. So I won't say I told you so because it wouldn't be so different even with anyone, even your precious Julius. A man is a man—they're not so different one from the other. One chases women and another chases horses and one has his nose in the Talmud and another wants to change the world, and whatever they do they claim they're doing it for us. But in truth whatever they do, they ignore us. Which is not so bad because when you come right down to it we don't really have very much in common with them.

All this wasn't exactly comforting, but Mama never was comforting and I couldn't talk about this with Papa, who sometimes could be. So Mama and I drank a cup of tea and she said, Marriage is really about kinder *and patted my belly, where Chaim Baer was already beginning to swell me up a little.* Children are more important than husbands, *she said, and touched my face, which felt odd because it was rare for Mama to touch anyone beyond a perfunctory kiss that would miss your cheek by six inches.* You'll have beautiful boys, *she said, and she was right, but who expected them* All *to be boys and not a single little girl. After Baby Seymour, may God forgive me, I was so sure the next one would be a girl that I secretly bought pink blankets and baby clothes and hid them away, and Lazar and I together picked a name that had nothing to do with any dead relative— Nancy—that we shared with our good friends.* Nancy with a tassel, *said Harry Friedman at the hospital, and much as I love that man I could have killed him when everyone laughed. But it was hardly his fault that it was another boy. Nor Lazar's either, not really; he said he wanted a girl this time, but I don't think they ever really want girls. Or is it us? Are we the ones afraid of daughters?*

So difficult was it to believe that Rabin was not a girl that for three years I refused to let his hair be cut, but only had it trimmed into a pageboy, and sometimes I would secretly put him into Nancy's little dresses when Lazar was not around. One Saturday Lazar suddenly says, Enough. He needs a haircut, *and drags him off to the Blue Bird Barber Shop. Two hours later he returns and my baby with the long brown locks is gone and in his place is a real little mensch saying,* Look at me, Mommy, look at me, *and I take him in my arms, but my heart is breaking because I know I have lost him like I have lost the others.*

Chaim Baer was the one really meant to be a girl. He might have been named for Lazar's father, but there's no doubt about it: he belongs to my family. He looks like Schloime as a baby, has Elliot's musical talent, and learned to read even before going to school, just like me. When he was at the breast, I would always hum to him and I would put his cradle in the living room right next to the piano and play Chopin, Liszt, and Brahms for hours while he smiled and gurgled. When he was four, I started him on piano lessons with Lily Gordon, who had been my first teacher too. Did he take to the piano? Like Elliot, music ran in his veins. Me, I always had to work hard, to practice, practice, practice until I got a piece down just right. Elliot never practiced. Just sat down and tore through whatever music you put in front of him. Chaim Baer was the same. When he was five, I knew I had a genius on my hands. At seven, a prodigy. At nine, he gave up the piano, and my heart broke. Sure he took it up again in his teens and now he can improvise and play jazz and all that, but he'll never be a real musician.

Who's to blame but Lazar. When Chaim Baer was around seven, he started: Practicing is fine, it's good to practice. But does he have to be inside all day long? Why isn't he playing ball with the other kids?

But Daddy, *he would say.* I don't want to play ball.

Lazar stormed around the living room. What do you mean you don't want to play ball. Get outside. Canadian kids play ball.

But Daddy...

No ifs, ands, or buts. I had to work as a kid; I never got to play. Not in Romania and not here. But it's different for you, you're lucky. You can play all you want. Now get outside and play.

Lazar, leave the boy alone, let him decide....

Don't you start, *he roared.* He's not a Kreisler, he's not sick, and he's not a pansy. He's a Rotenstein and Rotensteins make something of themselves. Rotensteins play ball.

The yelling had an effect. Chaim Baer tried to play with the other boys, but he had no skill, no enthusiasm, no coordination—even I could see that. Lazar too. So one day he brought home a set of boxing gloves.

Okay. He can't play ball. At least he can learn to defend himself.

Lazar, don't...

Chaim Baer, put on the gloves.

Daddy...

PUT THEM ON!

They went out into the yard and I locked myself in the bedroom. Even through the closed windows and drapes and the sounds of my own sobbing as I lay on the bed, I could hear Lazar yelling Hit me, hit me, *and Chaim Baer pleading,* Daddy, *and Lazar yelling louder. When I came out, Chaim Baer was in his room. Only at dinner did*

I see his bruised, unhappy face, but by that time I was too far away from all three of them to do more than silently serve the chicken soup and roast beef and apple pie. Lazar kept trying to talk about base-ball and politics, but Chaim Baer said nothing, and David was sub-dued, and I refused to open my mouth. Toward the end of the meal, Lazar became impatient and his eyes began to look that way: What's the matter—the cat got everyone's tongue?

Does anyone want seconds on pie? *I answered.*

He stood up, slammed his fist on the table, and banged out of the room. In bed that night, he tried to explain, saying over and over, A Jewish kid's got to learn to defend himself. *With my back turned to him, I refused to answer, refused any comment when he said,* It will be all right with Chaim Baer, you'll see, *refused to respond when he touched my shoulder. Not that it was so good between us before that, not that it had ever been so good between us, but I have refused to respond to him ever since.*

Lazar was dead wrong. It never again was all right with Chaim Baer. He took piano lessons for two more years, but never played with the same spirit as before. What I couldn't understand was why he drew away from me, as if the beating had been my fault. Before that we had been close as a mother and son could be—he was my Julius, my baby brother Schloime. We touched and hugged and laughed and played duets together. Now when I hugged him he did not hug back; when I kissed him he pulled away. Soon I stopped doing both, and we became like strangers; he was not mine, but somebody else's little boy, someone we were sheltering until his parents returned to claim him. When he gave up the piano, it no longer mattered much to me, no more than when David, who was completely tone deaf, gave it up after one year of lessons. And when Chaim Baer took up the pi-ano again and began to play jazz, it was Lazar who encouraged him. They say you learn from your mistakes: at least I never bothered to push the piano on Rabin.

Bobby Hall at the time of high school graduation. I envied him the height of his pompadour, a sign that he would go far.

NINE

Mixed-up Bobby

Tapes Raise Questions in Detective's Death

A premonition of death seemed to stalk the shadowy world in which Burbank private detective Robert Duke Hall plied his trade.

Bobby Hall was scared, obviously, with good reason.

"He carried a concealed weapon with him every place he went," said Carol Hall, his estranged wife.

"I think Robert Vesco is trying to kill me," Hall told his teen-age daughter when she asked why he was carrying a gun to their Father's Day dinner at a Burbank restaurant.

One of his closest friends, Lawrence P. Mathes, 42, also had noticed Hall's growing anxiety and fear.

"He loaded every gun in the house," Mathes, who had shared Hall's home for six months, told Burbank investigators. "He never answered the door without a gun in his hand."

The 44-year-old private detective was right about one thing—somebody was out to kill him.

Little more than a month after his cryptic explanation to his daughter, the slight, bearded Hall was dead.

He was killed at 11:10 p.m. July 22 by an unknown assailant who fired a single shot into the back of his head through the open kitchen window of his Burbank home, police said.

What made Hall, a relatively obscure operator in his own right, think that an international figure such as Vesco, fugitive financier and millionaire wheeler-dealer, would bother to reach out from his exile of his Costa Rican fortress to have him murdered?

The answer to that can almost certainly be found in Hall's association with Thomas P. Richardson, 37, convicted Century City stock swindler and a Vesco "protege" currently facing a six-year term in federal prison.

There is evidence to show that Hall was helping Richardson in an attempt to squeeze financial aid out of Vesco under the threat of giving federal prosecutors damaging information about the fugitive financier.

Vesco, who fled first to the Bahamas, then to Costa Rica, is under federal indictment on charges stemming from a secret $200,000 contribution he made to former President Richard Nixon's 1972 campaign in a reported attempt to quash a probe of his finances by the Securities and Exchange Commission.

But if Vesco really did want Hall dead, he was not the only one, according to investigators.

"Hell there were probably any number of people who wanted to see this guy dead, just by the nature of the kind of work he did," said Burbank Det. Lt. Al Madrid, who is heading the investigation.

"From what we know of his background ... the bugging ... the wiretapping ... the digging into other people's lives, he probably came up with some information he shouldn't have and it led to his death...."

Law enforcement officers from the local to federal level had known Hall for years in a variety of roles—as an informant, as a source for the illicit "happy shots" of speed and as someone to handle the unsavory, often illegal tasks of bugging and wiretapping.

While it's hard to find anyone with a complimentary word for Hall personally, even his most ardent detractors are vocal in praise of his talents for wiretapping and electronic eavesdropping.

LOS ANGELES TIMES, SEPTEMBER 10, 1976

W henever my cousin Bobby Hall got his name in the *Los Angeles Times*, the news was—with one exception—bad. Bad for Bobby. Bad for the family (or so everyone said). Bad for his young cousin Rabin (me), for I was always having to explain Bobby's brushes with the law to curious, uncomprehending friends whose fathers, unlike mine, all had regular employment. Fathers who were accountants, doctors, or the owners of small businesses such as Factor's Catering Service, where Rabin got his first real job, scraping clean plates made greasy by the chicken and stuffed kishke, the inevitable main course and side dish at those weekly Sunday night weddings of couples whose parents in the fifties still spoke with the accents of Eastern Europe. Fathers who knew nothing about the numbers or bookmaking or bootlegging or any of the other usual activities of my family.

Bobby's arrests—for that was the usual focus of the news stories—angered rather than surprised my relatives. In half a century of racketeering, he was the first member of the family to be arrested, let alone convicted. The first, that is, if you excluded Tilly's husband, sweet-talking Uncle Charlie, who did two years for setting fire to his failing upholstery business in order to collect the insurance. People were plenty upset about that too, but it wasn't as if he were working in one of the family trades. Besides, Charlie was a Hungarian, and a good guy who could hold his schnapps. But Bobby Hall was an American who smoked weed. Nobody in the family would ever think him a good guy, and only Rabin would ever enjoy having a drink with him.

What can you expect? said Lazar, the lifelong socialist. He could never forgive Bobby's father, Duke, for running Marathon Dances in the thirties, an enterprise that—unlike numbers or bookmaking—deluded and exploited members of the working class.

Hannah blamed everything on Bobby's mother, Clara, the daughter of Lazar's sister, Polly, who had come to California when her bootlegger husband went to work as a goon for studios that were resisting union attempts to organize Hollywood. Hannah had disliked Clara ever since Lazar had insisted she make a lunch for his niece when she first came to Montreal in 1929. Sixteen and every inch the flapper—short skirt, bobbed hair, cloche hat, rolled silk stockings—Clara smoked all through the meal, picked at every carefully prepared dish Hannah put before her—the chopped liver, the chicken soup with matzo balls, the stuffed cabbage, the roast brisket with potatoes—and finished by stubbing out her last cigarette in the homebaked apple pie with its à la mode topping.

Can you imagine anything more disgusting? Fifty years had not diminished Hannah's outrage.

Chaim Baer and David's shared dislike for Bobby was more direct. To young men raised in Montreal, Bobby was too much the Californian—loud, pushy, an insufferable braggart, a liar, unreliable, and dishonest. Not only did he think it his right as a second cousin to hit them up for twenty bucks with regularity, but each time he refused to acknowledge that he had not yet repaid the previous twenty.

Rabin was the only one in the family to mourn when the last and most sensational news stories about Bobby appeared during July 1976, in the weeks following his murder. As reported in the *Times*, he was shot through the head with a single bullet as he stood at the sink in the kitchen of his Burbank home drinking a glass of tap water. *Impossible,* thought Rabin, who after a few years in the antiwar movement was hip to the lies that found their way into the press. Bobby drinking straight gin or vodka. Bobby smoking a reefer, as they were still called when he first offered one to Rabin in 1949. Bobby popping brightly colored pills or cooking up something in a spoon while a syringe lay on the kitchen table. All these images were much more plausible than the one in the newspaper. Why, Bobby Hall wouldn't be caught dead with a glass of tap water in his hand.

The name of the killer was also a surprise: Jim Lebec, a muscular, health-food type whom Bobby had introduced to Rabin the week the Rotensteins arrived in California in October 1946. The two cousins had first met only a few months earlier, when Clara had come to Montreal with her son to see if anyone was willing to bankroll her two-bit bookmaker husband, the tall, slender (*long drink of water*—Lazar) and wholly ineffectual Willy Shapiro, into a larger operation. (Nobody was.) Among the cousins, Bobby won a quick reputation. Even Morty could not keep up with him. Together the two stole magazines and soft drinks from candy stores on the Main, sprinting away from outraged storekeepers and once outrunning a cop, tearing down streets and alleys, jumping over fences, crashing through backyards. Bobby ripped holes in three pair of good pants in two weeks and had a punch-out with a *brute* of a guy (Bobby's description) who did not like the idea of a fourteen-year-old barging through his rosebushes. Bobby's shiner was the envy of all his cousins. Sheila kept wanting to touch it, but Bobby pushed her away. *Rabin,* he said. *When you come to California, I'll show you how to have a* really *good time!*

Bobby's exploits were on my mind as Lazar drove the Packard, its generator needle off the dial to the right, into Los Angeles on October 12, 1946. To eyes accustomed to the dull red brick and gray stone of Montreal, the bungalows of green, pink, and white spoke of leisure, romance, wealth.

Is this the nice section of town? Rabin kept asking as they drove through Glendale, Eagle Rock, and Los Feliz.

Nah, nah. You ain't seen nothin' yet. Lazar was doing his Jimmy Durante imitation.

They pulled to a stop in front of a tiny yellow house with two palm trees in front, the tallest trees that Rabin had ever seen.

Sid and I planted them twelve years ago, said Polly, a recent widow, sniffling, *The day we moved in.*

All of them were standing in the yard, looking up—Polly, Clara, Lazar, Hannah, and Rabin. All except Bobby Hall, who was gesturing at Rabin with his shoulders and hands, as if to say, *Let's get outta here.* Half an hour later they were walking on Hollywood Boulevard, heading, at Rabin's request, toward the legendary corner of Vine, where, Bobby had insisted, there was *nothing but a bunch of pansies.* Was it that remark, or Bobby's swagger, or the fact that he took a pack of Camels from the back pocket of his jeans, stuck one cigarette behind his ear and lit another, or was it the way he shot off his mouth at everyone—the fat woman in the ticket booth at the miniature golf course on Sunset, the midget selling newspapers at the corner of Ivar and Hollywood, the old man with a cane tapping his way across the street against a red light on Gower, the hot-looking broad in the tight skirt walking into the coffee shop on Wilcox, the guy in a leather jacket roaring down Ridgewood on a motorcycle— just what was it that created the sense of menace, of incipient danger, that Rabin would always feel when with Bobby, from this first walk on a warm October day down to their last meeting on another warm October day sixteen years later, just after Rabin was discharged from the army, when they bumped into each other in a market on San Vicente and Bobby took his cousin back to his apartment near Brentwood Village, an apartment with nothing in the living room but a huge stereo system with enormous speakers and some large pillows where two women—girls, really, for they were still in their teens— one a blond and the other brunette, lounged in provocative poses and kept pouting like Playboy bunnies. Bobby and Rabin smoked dope and Bobby took a bottle of Beefeater Gin from the refrigerator and they passed it back and forth, and he asked how come a smart guy like his cousin, *the professor,* got caught by the draft, and Rabin told him exaggerated stories of what it was like to command an

M46A1 tank at Fort Knox, and even more exaggerated stories about the Black women picked up in the Crow Jim bars of Louisville, where he got in only because his buddy, Turpin, who played halfback for the Minnesota Vikings, put both of his huge fists on the bar and said in a threatening voice: *The ofay is with me!* And then Bobby spoke of his own days in the Coast Guard in San Diego, days spent mostly in the bars and brothels and gambling clubs of Tijuana, and when he learned that Rabin had received a Dear John letter from Sylvia on his twenty-sixth birthday, his patriotic cousin who was defending America's gold supply, not to mention the girls of America, from godless Communists, Bobby muttered *women, women,* and then waved toward the girls with a question in his eyes that Rabin answered by shaking his head—he would rather smoke and talk right now, for after all they hardly got to see each other anymore.

To tell the truth, they never saw each other very much, not after the Rotensteins' first months in Los Angeles—not more than once or twice a year. But starting in the early fifties, you could keep up with Bobby's exploits through the press. The earliest pieces were short, no more than two- or three-inch reports buried way at the back of the news section, next to items about how rabid coyotes were eating the pets of people who lived in Laurel Canyon and how joyous it felt for identical twins to be reunited after not seeing each other since their separation during the Russian Revolution of 1905.

RIFLE TOTING TEENS
SHOOT OUT LIGHTS
ON 6 BLKS OF SUNSET

TIRES SLASHED
BY STUDENTS
WHEN H'WOOD HI
LOSES BIG GAME

---

3 YOUTHS HELD IN
LIQUOR STORE HOLDUP—
CLAIM H'LLW'N PRANK

We might not have seen these headlines over stories that included, among others, Bobby's name, had not a weeping Clara phoned Lazar for consolation.

He's a good kid. His heart's in the right place. He just needs a real father. Willy's no father. He's hardly a husband. He doesn't know what to do with a kid.

A kid? snorted Lazar after he hung up. *He'll get our goat and soon be a jailbird.*

Rabin's father proved to be wrong. Bobby beat every rap—evidence turned out to be circumstantial; witnesses failed to appear or changed their minds; judges decided this teenager with the big smile and charming, if oily, manners was no hardened offender but only *mixed-up* or *misunderstood.* Such words were never applied to Rabin and his group (you could hardly call them a gang) of friends, not one of whom would be arrested until several years after graduating from college. In junior high they were ordered to stay away from Hollywood Boulevard at night by parents worried over reports that Wolf Packs, gangs of rough teenagers in leather jackets, owned the street. By the time they reached high school, the Wolf Packs had vanished from the press, and the group's idea of an exciting evening was to attend a feature film at Grauman's Chinese or the Pantages on its first night, or to listen for hours to records in the booths of Wallach's Music City at Sunset and Vine without ever purchasing anything, or to stand at the outdoor counter of the Hollywood Ranch Market, drinking coconut juice and furtively flipping through the girlie magazines on the rack.

Dishonesty, antisocial behavior, teenage rebellion—none of these were major factors in the lives of the guys on Rabin's block. Yes, everyone knew that Max filched dollar bills from the purse of his feeble, eighty-seven-year-old grandmother; and once Herb was punched out by a few guys on the football team who thought there was something funny about the way he always won during the Friday afternoon blackjack games played behind the shop building; and in his junior year Don was abruptly sent off to Black Fox Military Academy after he beat his ten-year-old brother so badly that he was rushed to the emergency room at Mt. Sinai Hospital for a bunch of stitches; and it was understood that if pills were missing from a bathroom cabinet, then Harry had been around, and when you went to visit him on Shabbas you would find him listening to Beethoven symphonies with a dazed expression, or if he played Ping Pong (the major Sabbath entertainment in his Orthodox household), he would often swing wildly or simply watch the ball go past him with a holy smile.

Rabin's only criminal actions came during the summer he and Mervyn got the odd idea they might win a reputation by becoming experts at golf, a game that nobody but parents or grandparents seemed to play. After two weeks of getting up early enough to catch the bus and tee off at the Griffith Park nine-hole course at eight o'clock, and after spending long mornings and longer afternoons thrashing through the underbrush, trying to find where their wild shots had gone, the sport began to seem far less exciting than stealing golf balls from the sports department at the Owl Rexall drugstore on the corner of La Cienega and Beverly, balls they cleverly concealed, six at a time, inside a portable radio from which the battery had been removed. What started as economic necessity soon became a nightly habit. By late August Rabin and Mervyn had enough golf balls to last a lifetime and were as bored with stealing as with golf. On the very evening they glanced at each other in the Rexall, silently acknowledging that the thrill was gone, and then turned away empty-handed from the display of golf balls, the two boys were seized by a house detective as they walked out of the store.

Lazar, who was just behind them, said, *Unhand those boys.*

Not on your life. They're thieves. The detective sounded outraged, but he let go of their arms. *Open the back of that radio. You'll see what I mean. They've got golf balls in there. You can't steal from Rexall.*

Mervyn complied. The back compartment was empty.

What did you do with them? His voice was lower. *They've been taking golf balls for weeks.*

You've got golf balls in the head! Lazar raised his voice. *This is false arrest. They're good boys.*

The detective slowly backed away. *They're not under arrest. But they should be. They've been stealing.*

Well, this isn't Nazi Germany. You can't arrest people without evidence.

The detective mumbled something that might have been an apology and fled back into the store. Lazar began to shake his fist and rave about the evils of big companies. Never again would he shop at Rexall, which he had, single-handedly, been supporting by spending thousands of dollars each week. They would hear from his lawyer the next day; they would hear from his congressman; they would hear from his senator. You couldn't go around grabbing honest citizens, not even kids, just because you had some crazy idea that they were stealing golf balls. Golf balls! Who would steal something stupid like golf balls? Why if his kid were going to steal something, he'd steal something valuable, not something idiotic like golf balls.

People coming out of the store were edging past the short, angry man toward their cars in the parking lot.

Dad. Come on. People are looking.

Lazar turned around, placed himself between Rabin and Mervyn, took each one by the arm just like the detective and led them toward the car. Just before they reached home, he said: *For Christ's sake, get rid of the damn golf balls right away just in case they send someone snooping around the house.*

Rabin and his friends might not indulge in antisocial behavior, but they didn't indulge in much social behavior either. In the first year of high school they became passionate about sports, religiously attending every Tuesday and Thursday basketball and every Friday afternoon football game, cheering loud and long for Fairfax High's generally hapless teams. (What could you expect from a school with a student body that was 98 percent Jewish? At least this: the Fairfax chess team regularly reached the state finals and won the championship title three times in the fifties.) Just as religiously, they avoided all noontime and after-school pep rallies, all sock hops and junior proms. On weekends they never went to the Hollywood Palladium to hear Les Brown's Band of Renown or The Rage, Miss Patti Page, and they only knew by reputation the far-off El Monte Legion Stadium, where on Saturday nights guys who hung around Auto Shop took girls with enormous hairdos to hear (apparently) Mexican bands perform Spanish-language rhythm and blues and (sometimes) to engage in fights with pachucos from East L.A.

During the all-important lunch hour, Rabin and his friends hung out on the front lawn together, eating tuna sandwiches and home-baked cookies from brown-bag lunches prepared by their mothers, while kids in leather jackets slipped across Melrose to grab hamburgers and fries at Mike's Big Burgers. From a distance they lusted across the grass after the clusters of heavily lipsticked girls in club sweaters and immaculate white bucks—the Tantras, tight-skirted and glamorous in black; the Cubadons, pleated and wholesome in pink; the Raynettes, knockouts in flaming red from head to toe. Their jealousy mounted when those beefy crew-cut guys with club jackets—Sheiks, Trojans, Grenadiers—lounged up to these goddesses, casually put their arms over their shoulders, and said things that made the girls laugh. Revenge came in feeble remarks about how guys with such thick heads and bad grades were poor prospects for college. It wasn't much comfort.

Of all the guys in his group, Rabin seemed (at least to himself) to be the shyest. He blushed whenever a cute girl in class said something in his direction, and he remained mute when encountering such a creature in the halls—even Sheila Staller, the only one of the Cubadons who seemed open and willing to talk to anyone. Sheila was so friendly that cadaverous Harry actually got up the nerve to ask her for a date for a Saturday night and was told, sweetly enough he reported, that much as she would love to go out with him she was unfortunately booked up on every Saturday until graduation two years hence.

By the end of the first year in high school, some of Rabin's friends were pulling ribbons from girls' hair, driving them home, asking them out on dates. But not Rabin, who specialized in unrequited (and unspoken, for he never shared his feelings with his most intimate friends) love for self-centered club girls with lacquered nails and perfect hairdos; girls who—had they acknowledged his existence—would surely have found him a creep; girls he did not approve of in public but in private considered beautiful beyond compare; girls he fantasized about in the most chaste way, imagining taking them to movies and holding their hands and kissing them goodnight on the cheek; girls he could not visualize kissing him, or anyone else, with their mouths open; girls whose breasts he could not imagine touching, even with a trembling hand; girls whose nipples he refused to let himself think about, just as he could not think about what they might have under their neat, pleated skirts and between their legs; girls who had never been fucked and would never be fucked, for what did Rabin know about fucking? Nothing really, nothing except what could be gleaned dimly from the pages of those pamphlets, one entitled *Man* (gray) and the other entitled *Woman* (orange), that he found one day in the bookshelf, hidden there by who: Chaim Baer? David? his father? his MOTHER?—pamphlets that talked explicitly and clinically about sex without telling him what he wanted to know, like where it was exactly on them and how it looked and how you put yours in hers, because just at the most important moment, just when he wanted specificity, the words grew vague and rhapsodic—*the man faces the earth because man is made of dust, the woman faces the sky of future generations that will spring from her womb.* And the dozens of diagrams, the line drawings, the cross sections with little arrows and Latin names might give a good sense of how things looked to a cartographer, but they were of no use whatsoever to a virgin who desperately wanted to get laid.

The only girl that Rabin both loved and talked to was Norma Overturf. She appeared one day during the middle of the term in Mr. Quick's World Literature class (Rabin's favorite) and was given the seat next to Rabin. Norma had long blond hair, messy and somehow inviting; a tight knit skirt and a very tight sweater; heavy makeup, bright lipstick, and a smell of perfume that from a desk away made Rabin feel faint. He was falling desperately even before she turned to him with a smile, and when she said (had he ever heard such a soft voice?), *Is this teacher tough?* and he answered without thinking, blushing, or choking, *Nah, if you're smart you know what he's going to ask on the tests,* and she replied, in a husky voice, *And I'll bet you're one of the smartest,* Rabin became her slave. At noon, when he saw Norma with a group of girls—not club girls, she was not a club girl, but, Rabin knew, fiercely independent just like him—he could not help pointing her out to Marshall. His friend glanced at Norma for a moment, licked his lips, and said, *Forget it, Rabin. Any girl that looks like that's bound to be a whore.*

After her arrival, Rabin sailed into World Lit each day ready to recite poems from memory, answer questions about Rabelais, Dickens, and Hemingway, fill in the blanks on snap quiz questions, and— above all—help Norma with assignments that could seem difficult, for after all she, poor kid, had arrived late in the term, and Mr. Quick, truth to tell, did not seem to like girls very much, at least he rarely called on them and never on her (which she did not, she said, mind), and he made plenty of disparaging remarks about *old maid* scribblers, people like Emily Dickinson and Charlotte Brontë, whose works were in the required textbook. Norma might not seem very smart, but Rabin knew that given a chance, she would be open to education and want to learn enough so that she could be just like him, a lover of great literature and a writer of great novels, or at least a reader of great novels, like the ones he would write and the first of which he would dedicate to her. Against all his principles, Rabin wrote answers for the final test on little pieces of paper and, during the exam, slipped them to Norma. His reward for her B plus—*It's the highest grade I ever got,* the softness of her voice dissolving in a squeal—was a kiss directly on the mouth, delivered in the hallway just after class, a kiss that left Rabin so weak that he forgot to do what he had been gathering his courage to do for eight weeks: ask her for a date.

Two weeks later, when school resumed for the spring term, Norma was gone. Rumors had it she had gotten pregnant from some older guy who was not in high school and her parents had sent her away to have the child, but they were the same rumors that went around when any girl suddenly left school. The difference in this case was that Norma Overturf was really unknown at Fairfax, a stranger who arrived one day and vanished another, without making—or so everyone said—any friends at all. Except for Rabin. But only he knew about that friendship, only he knew its depth, only he knew that behind the (yes, admit it) sluttish facade, Norma was a sweet, sensitive girl with a hunger for knowledge and great potential to become... to become...

None of Rabin's silent passions was greater than that for Rachel Nissenbaum, daughter of Dr. Sheldon (born Shmuel) Nissenbaum, longtime head of Temple Beth-Hollywood, a community leader regularly referred to in *Variety* as the *Rabbi to the Stars*. Rachel was so radiant (Homecoming Queen), intelligent (a straight-A student), and accomplished (she regularly played the Debussy piano *Nocturne* at school assemblies) that she reached the social heights without ever joining a club. But stardom had its perils. *You know about rabbi's daughters,* guys would say as she sailed by on the quad. *They're hot to trot.* Girls were no less vulgar, as Rabin was shocked to learn when he overheard Diana Pancyk, a Tantra, say, *She thinks her shit doesn't smell, but it stinks as bad as mine.*

More shocking was the sight one day after school of Rachel, strolling across the lawn, holding hands with Bobby Hall. While they stopped and faced each other, Rabin was struck by contradictory impulses—should he approach, flee, call out? Bobby solved the problem by waving and pulling Rachel toward him.

Meet my cousin, Rabin.

Hi.

H'lo, said Rabin.

What grade are you in?

Rabin's face felt hot and sweaty.

Ninth.

Oh, she said. *A sophomore.*

It grew hotter, sweatier.

He's the smartest guy in the family. Probably the smartest kid in the whole school—smarter even than you, sweetie. We're all going to know his name some day. Rabin Rotenstein. He's going to do big things!

Really! said Rachel, smiling sweetly at Bobby: *It's good to know somebody in your family has brains.*

After that, Bobby—still a senior at Hollywood High after four years—appeared at Fairfax almost every day, holding hands with Rachel, nuzzling her neck, stroking her hair, helping her into a sleek white Mercury convertible lowered to within four inches of the ground. Sometimes Rabin would spend a few minutes with them, hanging over the side of the car. Soon he could talk to Rachel without blushing, especially about serious things like books (they both liked Sinclair Lewis, especially *Main Street* because it showed, she said, *how much better things are for women now*) and music (they both liked Chopin and Liszt) and even politics (*Truman may not be FDR, but he's sure right about Israel!*). Bobby, who read nothing but the sports pages of the *Times* and always had his car radio blasting raucous *race records* broadcast by some Negro station on Central Avenue, presided over their conversations like a proud parent until he got bored, then revved up the engine and peeled away.

One afternoon Bobby waved Rabin into the backseat. Even in the open car, Rachel's scent was wonderful. They dropped her off for a music lesson and Bobby said, *Let's go to my place.* What a surprise to see that he did not live with Clara and Willy but had a room in an apartment with *some guys* who were no longer in high school. Everyone else Rabin knew lived with their parents. David, a PFC stationed at the Rocky Mountain Arsenal, had stayed at home during his four years at UCLA, sleeping in a bed next to the one that Chaim Baer, twenty-five and unemployed, rarely vacated, despite sporadic attempts by Lazar to shame him out of the house. Dramatically, Lazar would throw open the door of the bedroom, gesture grandly at the horrendous mess—the books, papers, magazines, and items of clothing piled on the bureaus, the desk, the nightstand, the chairs, and the floor—and shout, *What do you think this is, a pig sty? No,* answered Chaim Baer, rolling over and facing away from the door. *It's a bedroom and I'm sleeping.* Stuck for a meaningful answer, Lazar would retreat to the kitchen and berate Hannah, *Sooner or later I'm going to throw your lazy son out unless he gets a job.*

Bobby's room was a mess of barbells and weights and other exercise equipment and bodybuilding magazines with pictures of astonishingly muscular men on the covers.

Rachel, said Rabin. *She's quite something.*

Ah, she's just another slit.

But she's so beautiful.

Yeah, well, OK. But she's not that much.

Bobby offered Rabin a joint and a beer, and Rabin declined both.

Bobby smoked and put a new jazz LP, *The Lionel Hampton All Stars at the Pasadena Civic,* on his phonograph, and began doing handstands and then walking on his hands back and forth across the room.

Hey, Rabin, you should come see me compete.

At what?

Gymnastics, you dummy. Didn't you know I was one of the best in the city at Free Ex.

Free ex? Rabin had the haziest idea of gymnastics. Certainly it was not a sport anyone cared about or went to; gymnastics was as unpopular as his own sport, tennis, in which he had recently been humiliated 6–2, 6–1 on the first day of practice by a slender kid who looked about thirteen and played in his bare feet. The defeat became less painful when he learned that the kid was the son of one of the Hollywood Ten, which meant his family had already suffered a great injustice and deserved any breaks it could get. Why couldn't his cousin have taken part in a real sport, say, football or basketball? Even baseball would be OK.

Yeah, Free Ex.

What's it like?

Sort of like calisthenics put together into a kind of dance. It takes a lot of strength and balance. Come see me. I'm gonna be in the city finals in May.

Sure, said Rabin, hoping Bobby would forget about it by then.

They spent other afternoons at Bobby's apartment over the next months, listening to jazz while Rachel took piano lessons. Once Rabin attempted to smoke, but he coughed so much that he couldn't get high, so usually he drank half a beer and listened to Bobby talk about exploits that involved guns and switchblades and pranks that crossed the line into minor crime and put his cousin just one step ahead of the law. Rabin was surprised on the day Bobby said he was probably soon going to join the Coast Guard.

What for?

It's better than the draft. With the Coast Guard I can stay close to home, probably stay in Long Beach, and I can get into electronics school. I'm kinda interested in electronics—and maybe I can get a step toward engineering school. That might surprise some people, no?

Yeah. Rabin could not see Bobby as an engineer any more than he could see himself as one. After some special aptitude test, his parents had been called in by a school counselor and told that Rabin should prepare himself for this field because the country needed all the engineers it could get to help ward off the Communist menace, and not so many people had the math skills that their son had, and besides, for engineers employment was always guaranteed. Rabin hated the idea, but for some weeks Hannah and Lazar kept at him: *Listen to your teachers. You've got to have an education to get ahead in the world.*

Yeah, I'm going to college but I don't want to be an engineer.

You could do worse, said Lazar.

The pressure from home had two results: Rabin received his lowest high school grade, a C, in Advanced Algebra, and his parents were summoned to school again, this time to see the vice principal, who could not understand why a good student like their son had said in a loud voice in front of an entire classroom, *Fff——you,* to the sweet, elderly woman who was his math teacher.

Fff——you? asked Lazar, whose hearing was, he had begun to fear, going bad.

You know, said the vice principal.

No, I don't, said Lazar, turning to Hannah, *What's Fff——*

It's a very bad word, said Hannah, whose face was red.

Oh, I get it. You mean Fu—

Shaa, interrupted his wife.

For Rabin the expletive had been a kind of insurance, one that became necessary after his attempt to fail the class had not quite worked. Engineers, he was certain, did not say *fuck you* in public.

Rabin barely knew that Bobby was in the Coast Guard before he was out. Headlines on page 7 of the *Times* told us even before Clara called Lazar to complain about Willy. The articles were murky in their details, but the general drift was that a group of Coast Guard cadets (Bobby was one of five) had been discharged in connection with the disappearance—no theft could be proved—of a great deal of electronic equipment. They were not court-martialed either for lack of evidence or, the articles hinted, because of the possible implication of some higher officers.

Nine months later, Rabin attended Bobby's wedding to a girl named Bunny in a posh but small affair—forty guests consisting only of family and close friends—at Romanoff's, the most expensive restaurant in Beverly Hills. Bunny was rich and attractive enough beneath all the makeup and jewelry, but not much out of the ordinary if you took time to try to talk to her, which Rabin did. She had nothing to say about books or music or even sports. Bunny looked at Bobby steadily and worshipfully all through the dinner and the toasts and the comedic reading of telegrams from relatives all over the country, but her gray-haired parents could not conceal their expressions of terror, a result, perhaps, of the mistaken rumor whispered through the banquet hall that Bunny was four months gone. Or maybe they just did not like the idea of a suspected thief becoming part of their family circle.

Long before the wedding, we had all heard that Rachel Nissenbaum had been sent to a conservatory in Switzerland, and Bobby repeated the news to Rabin during their only moments alone that afternoon. They were standing drunkenly next to each other in the men's room, first at the urinals, then staring with bloodshot eyes into the mirror over the sinks, and Rabin was trying to offer congratulations that he didn't much feel.

Yeah, I know, said Bobby. *You wish it was Rachel. So do I. I really loved her. She could have helped me.*

Helped you what?

Ah, Rabin. She made me feel I had a chance.

It took more than another decade for Bobby to make it to the front page of the Metro section of the *Times*. By then, Rabin really was a professor, late-sixties style. He grew his hair to his shoulders, drove regularly to San Francisco to march against the war, meet women, score great dope, and dance to the Grateful Dead, and delighted in making self-righteous speeches to vast, noisy audiences. Politics provided Rabin with a unique perspective, for when Bobby was arrested for fraud, he was the only one in the family to find his cousin's activities a fitting blow against the corrupt beneficiaries of a corrupt economic system.

The scam for which Bobby was arrested had been neat and simple. With much publicity, he and some buddies opened a lot in Culver City that specialized in those luxury automobiles of the day, Cadillacs. Advertisements promised that they would pay the highest prices in town for clean used cars. The people who rushed to make a major profit off their Caddys found themselves fast-talked into taking a small amount of cash and a large promissory note for the rest payable in sixty days. There was one catch: by the fifty-ninth day all the cars had been sold off and the lot was closed. Bobby's radical anarchist blow against the system (for so Rabin could interpret his actions) might have worked had not the heavy hand of police authority dogged his organization and obtained evidence with a promise of immunity from prosecution. The newspapers did not report the identity of the finger man, but the money (most of it) was returned, and Bobby walked free.

His final appearances in the papers came shortly after Rabin returned from a year of living and teaching in Japan. The murder made front-page headlines for a couple of weeks, and major stories kept appearing about this complicated and mysterious crime for many months. Evidence pointed to Bobby's connection to major figures in politics and entertainment. He was, the newspapers reported, a licensed private detective and an expert in electronics. His specialty was wiretapping. He possessed tapes of compromising conversations involving Hollywood celebrities and underworld figures and government officials, including people like Frank Sinatra, Peter Lawford, members of the Kennedy clan, and Richard Nixon's friend, the financier Robert Vesco, a fugitive from justice currently rumored to be living somewhere in Central America. Lots of these people, journalists speculated, would have good reason to get rid of Bobby. The murder did not, in fact, surprise members of the police departments of either Burbank or Los Angeles, and nobody but journalists expressed much interest—and this only for a few weeks—in uncovering the deeper connections in the case. To read between the lines of the stories was to feel that just about everyone was happy to have Bobby out of the way—except perhaps his second wife and his daughter, who vanished from the papers after the first week.

The single time that newspapers reported good news about my cousin Bobby Hall had been years earlier, during the spring of my first year in high school, when I went to watch the City Championships in gymnastics. Bobby's second-place performance in Free Exercise received one sentence on page 9 of the next day's Sports section. Three decades later, when TV had made gymnastics international, Rabin would come to have a retrospective inkling that what Bobby had been doing thirty years before was beautiful. But at the time his graceful and strong performance, which took place in a gymnasium sparsely peopled with the families and friends of the participants, only baffled Rabin. What he really appreciated that day was Rachel sitting next to him, the beauty of her profile, and the expression on her face. During the two hours they sat side by side, Rabin knew for certain that everything was going to turn out just fine. Rachel and Bobby would get married, and somehow he would marry Rachel too, and they would all live happily ever after.

Lionel and Boris, a few years before they were separated by their parents
and taken to opposite ends of the world.

TEN

Izzy the Red

My Bar Mitzvah Speech

Dear parents, brothers, grandparents, relatives, friends, and members of this holy congregation,

I read today to you on the occasion of my Bar Mitzvah a portion out of the book of the prophet Jeremiah. It starts with a confession of the prophet. It runs as follows, "God is my strength and my stronghold and my refuge in the day of affliction." That confession was the result of his personal experiences and expressed his viewpoint of how man and mankind should shape their own destiny. He was convinced that an individual and a nation could often be the architects of their own fortune. In the year 626 B.C. he had been appointed by God to be a prophet to his people and mankind. He had the hardest struggle imaginable and was always in great danger. He would have broken down in complete despair but his confidence in God gave him strength again and again. He wanted the Jewish people to rely upon God and not upon that foreign power. For example: They should not depend upon Egypt which tried to entice them to rebel against the Babylonian Empire of which they were a satellite. He said: "Blessed is the man that trusts in the Lord and whose trust the Lord is."

From its history the Jewish people may learn how right the prophet was. All our alleged friends in the world did not prevent the unspeakable tragedy which has overwhelmed our people in Europe. The prophet warned us, "Cursed is the man that trusts in man and makes flesh his arm."

The Jewish people shall stick to God and obey the will of God.

What does God want man to be? God himself is righteousness and mercy, and demands of man to be just and kind.

I will be fair and never depart from the path of justice. I will be helpful to the needy as much as I can. By doing that I shall honor the name of my parents.

In that spirit I have been brought up by my good parents. I am grateful to them for that and for all they have done for me. I will be a good son and a faithful brother.

I pray to God that he in his mercy may hold his hand upon my good parents, brothers, and grandparents. God bless my relatives, friends and give peace to the Jewish people and all men of good will. God protect the new state of Israel.

Amen   DELIVERED BY RABIN ROTENSTEIN

FAIRFAX TEMPLE, MAY 1949

Uncle Izzy was a tailor, a member of a union, a freethinker, an atheist—and an outspoken Communist. He never went to synagogue, not even on the High Holidays, and he believed in free love, and *free whatever else he can get his hands on,* Grandma Freda would say. Everybody knew that Izzy was not the only person in the world with such beliefs, but other people had the decency to keep their opinions to themselves. How Freda hated to admit that her beautiful red-haired younger sister Henrietta was married to a man with such big ears and such a weird look in his eyes and such crazy ideas about politics, religion, and—let's face it—sex too. They lived way out there in the Maritimes, in St. John's, New Brunswick, and when Henrietta came to Montreal for a visit, Freda could see the bruises when her sister undressed for bed, but she never said anything about them after that first time when Henrietta laughed off her anxieties and confided in a voice that had no trace of shame, *But it's exciting when he's rough.* She paused: *Freda, maybe if you and Adolph*—but her older sister cut her off. On any such topic, the less said the better.

Izzy might be a Marxist who believed in the iron laws of History, but that did not stop him from taking the Depression personally. *It may be a way of squeezing the working class, but it's also a way of squeezing me.* What kind of a world was it where even a skilled tailor was thrown out of work? *Maybe if you went to fewer meetings and didn't make so many speeches and paid more attention to getting your orders filled they wouldn't have laid you off,* said Henrietta, but he began to raise his fist and she said no more. Henrietta had to be worried. She and the boys were almost starving despite the packages that Freda sent from Montreal every couple of weeks. She wanted to help out, but a lingering bourgeois sensibility made Izzy fly into a rage every time Henrietta suggested going to work as a maid or laundress. *My wife, handle the* schmutz *of the bourgeoisie! Better to starve!*

Henrietta was plucky, but she had her limits. There is good evidence she was in some ways relieved when Izzy announced he was going back to the Russia his parents had taken him from before the Revolution, back to the Workers' State where there was no unemployment and no Cossack-like Mounted Police in their red jackets, wading in to break up union meetings and demonstrations. Soon enough the Borozovitch family, on a freezing February day, stands on the docks in Montreal, everyone wearing dark coats and hats, and steam rises from their mouths with each breath, each word. On this dock there are no brass bands, no streamers, no cheering crowds. A rusty Soviet freighter looms over the small group, the families of a half dozen middle-aged men, eyes bright with alcohol and unadmitted fears. People shout, laugh, cry, but none of the Borozovitch group has much to say. Izzy, Henrietta, fifteen-year-old Lionel, and twelve-year-old Boris stare at each other, and it is up to the only other member of the family present, Lazar, to make conversation. He has driven them all to the docks in his black Pierce-Arrow. Clad in a cashmere coat, a silk scarf, and a gray fedora, Lazar makes a try at conversation: *Izzy, I admire you. You are a brave man to try such a new world.* Does he believe these words? Lazar's own flirtation with socialism is long past, but there remains a certain amount of open territory in his heart and he is capable of the occasional grand gesture—as long as it doesn't cost him too much. Lazar slips Izzy several fifty-dollar bills: *Call it a donation to the Revolution.*

When he first learned about his father's role in these proceedings, Rabin was not surprised. For years Lazar's leftist rhetoric—rancor?—

had flavored every family dinner. Three hungry boys seated at the breakfast room table, Hannah hovering over the nearby stove, smells of roast meat and potatoes and fresh-baked pies wafting through the room, and Lazar, the radio turned up loud, refuses to let anyone eat before the news is finished. *Ah, there's good news tonight!* That's the way it always begins, the voice of Gabriel Heatter rising and falling like the circus barker or con man he once must have been, the emphasis shifting from word to word depending on the topic, the mood, the season. What good news? That Senator McCarthy had exposed hundreds of more Communists. That President Truman had at last done something right by nationalizing the leftist railroad unions and sending the radicals back to work. That America had already doubled its nuclear arsenal and would double it again in three years. That our boys had pushed the North Koreans back to the Yalu River. That General MacArthur, that greatest of American military men betrayed by a weak and vacillating president, had moistened every eye in Congress when he ended his farewell address: *Old soldiers never die, they just fade away!*

During the broadcast, Lazar's blue eyes flashed and he muttered, *Fascist! Anti-Semite! Nazi!* As the last tones of the good news faded away, he snapped, *Turn the goddamn thing off!*, grabbed a kaiser roll, and angrily tore it in half while Hannah rushed steaming bowls and plates heaped with food to the table. *Dad, why do you listen if it makes you so mad?* The question regularly came from Rabin. *I'm not mad, it's the world that's mad* was the reply that started the usual tirade against the Big Interests, a group that included but was not necessarily limited to bankers, Republicans, Nazis, Henry Ford, the steel industry, Standard Oil, generals of the army and the air force, Germans, British diplomats, Hungarians, J. Edgar Hoover, Parnell Thomas, as well as most lawyers, stockbrokers, politicians, leaders of the B'nai Brith, and undertakers, particularly one named Paperman who had sold Lazar an enormously expensive family plot in Montreal without telling him that it could neither be resold nor, Lazar had just learned, be given to anybody else in the family. *He's a goniff! All of them. Undertakers and rabbis too. They're all goniffs!*

Talk about the Big Interests made Rabin feel angry and helpless.

They were always doing things to us, and we had no way of protecting ourselves, let alone getting back at them. Besides, what did his father know? He spoke with an accent. He could barely write. In school Rabin was studying American history, learning about the orderly processes of representative government and the American Way, the neat division into local, state, and national branches, the fair elections, the checks and balances, the tradition of political and social reforms, and the great champions of the people like Lincoln and Fiorello La Guardia and FDR. A government of, by, and for the people knew how to take care of the Big Interests when they got out of line. Lazar would have none of such arguments: *Oh, sure, that's what they want you to think. You think they let teachers tell the real truth? They'd all be fired!*

During the late forties and early fifties certain events seemed to signify that his father's fears were not wholly unfounded. One evening Hannah and a friend who was a librarian went off to Gilmore Field, a rickety wooden structure where Rabin spent summer Sunday afternoons watching doubleheaders of the Hollywood Stars, a perpetual second-division finisher in the Pacific Coast League, and consuming large quantities of peanuts, hot dogs, and Bireley's noncarbonated fruit drinks. Neither Hannah nor her friend were baseball fans. The evening at Gilmore was devoted to pleas for political and monetary support for the Hollywood Ten, a group of brave men who, Hannah reported with uncharacteristic passion, had done no more than refuse to answer the illegal questions of a congressional committee about their political beliefs—beliefs guaranteed as sacred by the Bill of Rights and the Constitution. To Rabin the words did not sound like any his mother would normally use. Hannah did not pay much attention to politics or newspapers. She preferred to read *classics,* a word she always uttered with a slight smile. As far as Rabin could tell, this meant biographies of Napoléon, romances by Daphne du Maurier, and mysteries by Erle Stanley Gardner or Ellery Queen.

Troubling issues also intruded into that new centerpiece of family life, the television set. Lazar's increasing thriftiness meant that the Rotenstein family was the last on the block—on any block!—to get a set. For years Rabin had to rush through Tuesday dinner and hurry over to Max Lipsky's house, arriving just as the four men in service station uniforms would begin singing a verse he would be able to remember fifty years later: *We are the men of Texaco, We work from Maine to Mexico, There's nothing like this Texaco of ours. Our show tonight is powerful, we'll wow you with an hour full of howls from a bower full of stars. We are the Texaco men. Tonight we may be show-men, tomorrow we'll be servicing your cars.* Then the curtain would open and there, sometimes in glorious drag (though we had never heard the word), was Uncle Miltie!

Only when Lazar was able to get a *deal* from a friend did Rabin's family finally acquire a TV. It arrived on a Saturday afternoon, a huge, light wooden console with doors that you opened to reveal a thirteen-inch screen—a round screen. They switched it on to the UCLA–St. Mary's football game, hoping to catch a glimpse of David in the rooting section. The picture was so gray that it was difficult to tell the difference between the presumably light-shirted visitors and home team Bruins. Lazar began to brag: *Now wasn't that worth waiting for? I'll bet none of your friends have such a big screen!* Rabin was not convinced. *But it's round, Dad. Nobody has a round screen. I've never seen a round screen. It cuts off the corners. You don't see the whole game!*

Every time Rabin wanted something important, his father would get similar sorts of *deals.* When he ached for one of those neat little 45 rpm record players with the big round plastic spindles, Lazar after months of making calls to important *friends,* produced a bulky, portable three-speed Webcor changer (so heavy that Rabin could not move it without the help of one of his brothers) covered in some sort of red figured plastic that was supposed to resemble leather. The slender spindle could only play 45s if you slipped a special alumi-num adapter onto the record, and the first few times Rabin tried to do so, he cracked the vinyl, then stormed into his father's room, de-manding that he pay for a new record. It was worse with the leather jacket. All the kids in Auto Shop and on the teams and in the clubs had black leather jackets with lots of evil-looking zippers and silver snap buttons. Lazar managed to come up with something slightly different—a simpler style with a knitted collar and cuffs and a discreet single zipper down the front. Oh yes, it wasn't quite the right color—it was powder blue. *Daddy,* Rabin wailed, *I can't wear a blue leather jacket to school.* Lazar was direct: *You asked for leather, you got leather. Leather is leather.* In the many years it hung in his closet, Rabin put on the jacket a single time, on a Sunday evening when the whole family was going to dinner at Wan Q. His reason was very practical: Lazar made it clear that if he didn't wear the jacket at least once, he would never receive an allowance again.

TV on weeknights was fun—*Time for Beany* with Cecil the Seasick Sea Serpent scrunching up his mouth and submerging just before the arrival of Captain Huffenpuff; *Rocket Patrol,* in which Commander Kit Corey dashed about the universe in a clearly cardboard spaceship; Liberace, with his shit-eating grin, sequined jackets, candelabra, and mediocre piano playing; *Dragnet,* in which Joe Friday showed that you didn't ever have to raise your voice either to get *just the facts, ma'am* or to catch the criminals. Sundays presented a more somber reality. *Omnibus,* hosted by the very British Alistair Cooke, who introduced scenes from Greek dramas, in which crazed women tore their hair, ranted, and slaughtered their children, their husbands, and themselves, or who utilized his own cultured accent to intone Dylan Thomas's poem for his dying father while the screen carried the image of a candle flickering against darkness. At the end of the last line—*Rage, rage, against the dying of the light*—the candle mysteriously snuffed out. This, we knew, was Art!

The political programs continued the darkling mood. On *Meet the Press* a national leader was challenged by an outspoken panel of journalists, the most outspoken, voluble, and vitriolic of whom was Lawrence Spivak, editor of the *American Mercury.* Rabin had never heard anyone speak so viciously. Spivak made no attempt to hide his hatred of leftists, labor leaders, diplomats, New Dealers, Fair Dealers, the American Civil Liberties Union, the NAACP, One Worlders, the United Nations, and the League of Women Voters, of fancy-pants Dean Acheson, who had lost China, and Walter Reuther, who had sold out honest working men, and the Rosenbergs, who had given away the secret of the bomb, and Harry Truman, who was preparing to hand the nation over to Joe Stalin on a platter. Socialists and Communists? They were beyond the pale, our mortal enemies in a twilight struggle for World Domination. Only a few men stood between us and total annihilation, brave warriors like Richard Nixon, unafraid to call a Commie a Commie, and Joe McCarthy, with his long lists of traitors in the State Department, and Whittaker Chambers, the Russian spy turned patriot, who hid microfilm in a hollow pumpkin and exposed the Hiss ring and the extensive spy operations of the Russians and their stooges all over America. Spivak was clear: America was soft and getting softer. The only thing that could save us were bigger defense budgets, more Superfortresses, more aircraft carriers, more A-bombs, more internal vigilance in rooting out the rotten elements of society, the parlor pinkos, the lefties, the fellow travelers, the college professors who corrupted our youth.

Lazar had a simple test by which to judge politics (or almost anything else): *Is it good for the Jews?* To Rabin this seemed odd, for his father was not a religious man. In Montreal he had belonged to the Sha'ar Hashomayim, the most elegant temple in Westmount, but rarely did he appear there on more than a single one of the three holiest days of the year. The rest of the time one of his sons had to accompany Hannah to services on Rosh Hashanah or Yom Kippur. After they arrived in California, Lazar refused to join a temple on the grounds that here they were *too expensive.* His humiliated wife was reduced to cadging tickets to the High Holidays from whichever friends that season had sick husbands or teenage kids in the process of rejecting the family heritage. What a surprise when Lazar sat Rabin down for a man-to-man talk just after his twelfth birthday.

It's time to begin studying for your bar mitzvah.
My what?
You heard me.
We don't even belong to a temple.
You'll study for a few months with a rabbi.
I don't want to study with a rabbi.
Who wants to study with a rabbi? You'll get lots of presents.
Do I have to?
Rotensteins get bar mitzvahed. You can't disappoint your mother.

For the next year Lazar drove his son two evenings a week to the dimly lit apartment of a frail but somehow frightening old European man who had food particles in his long beard, very strong breath, and—you could see when hot weather had him wearing shortsleeves—a long string of numbers tattooed on the inside of his left arm. Even after Lazar explained to Rabin what these numbers were, he found it difficult to feel sympathy for a man who drilled him mercilessly hour after tedious hour in the task of learning by rote the ten-minute passage of the Torah that he would have to read aloud to the congregation. Only once did Rabin dare stop the relentless proceedings with a question: *Rabbi, what do these words mean? What am I saying?* The old man stared through thick glasses at Rabin for a long time as if he had never seen him before and answered in a thick accent: *Mean? What should it mean? It means you should study harder. It means you're a Jew!*

The ceremony took place in a dingy storefront temple on Fairfax Avenue. Aside from immediate family and a few friends of his parents, the hall was filled with men who resembled the Hebrew teacher, men who bobbed and weaved when they prayed and looked up at Rabin, mangling their sacred tongue, as if he were a side of bacon. The performance ended with the Bar Mitzvah Speech, in theory the thoughts of the boy, but in this case dictated by his teacher and then tapped out by Rabin on Hannah's typewriter. Half a century later it remained pasted into a family album, misspellings, typing mistakes, and last-minute interpolations in pencil. It begins with the warnings of the prophet Jeremiah against trusting in nations rather than in God—*all of our alleged friends did not prevent the unspeakable tragedy which has overwhelmed our people in Europe*—then goes on to make promises: I will be fair, and just, a good son and a faithful brother. The speech concludes with a prayer that God bless his parents, grandparents, relatives, friends, members of the congregation, the Jewish people, and all men of good will. Written in pencil, but not in Rabin's youthful scrawl, just before the *Amen* is somebody's (the Hebrew teacher's?) afterthought: *God protect the new state of Israel.*

Despite the *mitzvah* of the ceremony—the praise of the rabbi (who promised to give a Bible as a present but never delivered), the prayers of the congregation, and the blessings of a Higher Power—Rabin would not step into a temple again until the bar mitzvah of his nephew, twenty-two years later. Nor would he ever again attend a holiday or Sabbath service. Could it have been the disappointing haul of presents: a few pen and pencil sets; a variety of books he would never open, books on Jewish holidays, on Jewish rituals, on Jews in history, and on Jews in sports; a daily diary for the year 1949 (now half over); several ill-fitting rayon shirts; a slightly used, inflatable beach ball; a deck of playing cards with pictures of famous Jews on the back; a small portable radio that broke down a few months later; and—most welcome—cash gifts that totaled $180. With this capital, Rabin wanted to open a savings account, but Lazar had a better idea: he would keep the money for his son so that Rabin could instantly obtain whatever amount he wanted when he wanted it. That this idea was far better in theory than in practice became evident a few weeks after the bar mitzvah, when Rabin asked for ten dollars.

What do you want it for?

What do you mean what do I want it for? It's my money.

I just want to make sure you don't spend it foolishly.

But it's my money.

I'm your father. It's my job to keep you from being foolish.

It's MY money. I need ten dollars.

Don't raise your voice to me, young man.

Daaad, geeez. I want to buy a new mitt.

You have a mitt. I just bought you one.

That was three years ago. I need a NEW mitt!

When I was your age we didn't even have mitts. We played with our bare hands.

C'mon, Daad, you never played baseball.

Don't tell ME what I played.

I WANT a MITT.

You think I didn't want a mitt? I had to go to work to support the family when I was twelve. We had no time for mitts.

It never got much better. Acting as if the money belonged to him, Lazar treated all requests as a kind of imposition, a drain on his time and resources. Even after he stopped asking why Rabin needed money, father and son continued to wrangle over just how much of the $180 had been spent. The problem was an ill-defined sense of what was part of normal parental economic obligation. When Rabin asked for money for books, or a new tire for his bicycle, or for renting a tenor saxophone and taking lessons with a music teacher, Lazar might say:

Okay. But it's coming out of your bar mitzvah money.

Dad, other kids don't pay for their music lessons.

We'll make a deal. You pay for the rental, I'll pay for the lessons.

No fair. If I didn't have any money, you'd pay for the whole thing.

But you DO have the money.

When he graduated high school in 1953, Rabin presented Lazar with a statement showing that there was still $75 in the account. His father pushed the paper away: *Don't be ridiculous. I've paid you the money ten times over.*

· ·· ——— ————

Neither Cousin Lionel nor Cousin Boris had the burden of worrying about bar mitzvah ceremonies or money or baseball mitts. They believed that organized religion and capitalist sports such as baseball were opiates of the masses. Like their father, Izzy, the two brothers were Communists; unlike him, Lionel and Boris joined and became active members of the Party. This similarity despite the fact that the two brothers were raised in different countries, half a world apart. Following the farewell on the Montreal docks in the mid-thirties, Lionel and Boris would not exchange a spoken or a written word for more than thirty years. They would not meet again face to face for almost four decades.

Blame Henrietta. Or praise her. Lionel was often uncertain which judgment was more appropriate. She and he were supposed to follow Izzy and Boris as soon as they got settled. But Izzy had greatly misjudged the need of the Workers' State for middle-aged tailors. Months of effort made him feel lucky to find a tiny bedroom with a window on an air shaft, in a communal apartment in which twelve people shared a bathroom and a kitchen that had a wood burning stove and no refrigerator. Father and son slept together in one bed until Boris went into the army five years later. Izzy remained in the same room until his death in the mid-fifties.

If Izzy had obtained one of the former czar's apartments in the Kremlin, it would have made no difference to Henrietta. She might be the freethinker of the Voss family, she might enjoy sex, associate with gentiles, and be sympathetic to ideas of social and economic equality, but twenty years of marriage to a man who lived on promises of a better future was more than enough. Still, Henrietta was not cruel. In the letters she regularly wrote to Izzy giving news of Lionel and the growing labor movement in Canada, she did not mention that before packing up and moving to Montreal, she filed papers in St. John's asking for a divorce on the grounds that her husband had abandoned her. When provincial officials learned that he had gone to the Soviet Union, they were happy to speed through the divorce of a woman who had been so obviously wronged.

Henrietta got a job at the Windsor Hotel as a maid. Before long she was a supervisor who could afford a small one-bedroom apartment off the Main. Lionel finished high school near the top of his class, but he spurned the idea of college as bourgeois and, after kicking around at a few odd jobs, went to work on the assembly line of Canadair, the largest aircraft company in the country. The job came through the good offices of his comrades in the Communist Party, which controlled the unions. By the time Canada entered the war right after the signing of the Stalin-Hitler pact, Lionel was a minor supervisor whose task it became, surreptitiously, to slow down production. With the German invasion of the Soviet Union in June 1941, that policy dramatically reversed. For the rest of the war he was happy to ride roughshod over democratic union opposition in order to enforce the No Strike–Win the War pledge that the Party had made. His sensitive job in military production meant that Lionel enjoyed a permanent deferment from the military draft.

Boris was not so lucky, but in the Soviet Union it was rather more difficult to avoid the army than in Canada. He probably would not have wanted an exemption. Boris hated Nazis, and he loved his new homeland almost as much as he loved music. Being short, undernourished, slightly tubercular, and a promising musician did not keep him out of the army, where he surprised himself by proving to be a natural leader. During the Battle of Moscow, he was commissioned on the battlefield and for several weeks commanded an infantry company that held against all enemy assaults. A splatter from a .50-caliber German machine gun put him in the hospital, where for many months he hovered between life and death. The wounds that took him out of the war provided certain benefits. He was welcomed into both the Academy of Music and the Communist Party, and after graduation went directly into the Composer's Union, a position that would insure him a decent living no matter what degree of talent he had at creating new music.

· · —— —— ——

The first time Rabin was called a Communist he laughed right into the face of the wide-eyed, blond sorority girl who had just used the epithet. *Only Communists are against the Greeks. We're the backbone of American democracy.* They were standing in the entrance hall of the Kappa Alpha Theta House, where Rabin was waiting for Celeste to descend from her room. Here he was an easy target, a vulnerable one, for this was not a venue where he could easily engage in political argument. Like many others too polite to mention it to his face, Celeste's *sister* was appalled at what Rabin was writing in the pages of the UCLA *Daily Bruin,* a publication whose editors were believed to be plotting the downfall of the fraternity and sorority system. Well, maybe they were. Rabin's target was the Restrictive Clauses in the Greek charters. His argument was simple: organizations that utilized state facilities and funds should not be allowed to function under charters that denied the equal access to people of (as they used to say) all races, creeds, and colors.

Such editorials were not his first subversive activities. These had begun in high school when, during the first Eisenhower administration, the pledge of allegiance to the flag was altered by adding the words *under God.* To Rabin this was a clear violation of the separation of church and state—*Why should an atheist be prevented from pledging allegiance?*—and he voiced his opposition by conspicuously refusing to say those two words during the pledge at school

Izzy the Red 171

assemblies. As a freshman at UCLA, Rabin had given five dollars (a week's allowance!) to the *Joe Must Go* movement, started by a Wisconsin newspaper editor who wanted to get Senator McCarthy recalled, and had for weeks worn its symbolic green feather pinned to his shirt. The next year he appeared at a rally for the twenty-one professors whose refusal to sign a special disclaimer oath, affirming they were not Communists, had led to their being fired by the university. He also voiced (though not in print) deep suspicions of the underlying intent of the Campus Crusade for Christ, an organization that managed to get a goodly number of football players and other jocks to renounce beer and to pledge in public their 100 percent Americanism. If they had listened closely, friends might have heard him whisper under his breath words that he would never say aloud: *Is it good for the Jews?*

The struggle over the Restrictive Clauses might be a serious business, but it was also fun. After he wrote several editorials denouncing university officials for siding with the Greeks, a rumor came back through an editor who was a stool pigeon for the administration that a dean who was scheduled to appear as a friendly witness before the House Un-American Activities Committee was prepared, if Rabin did not modify his language, to name him to the committee. Was the threat genuine? Rabin hoped so. His next editorial was the strongest yet—*The Iron Fist* invoked Franklin, Jefferson, and Lincoln, the Declaration of Independence, and the Bill of Rights, as it pilloried the chancellor's office for threats against students who were exercising the rights of free speech. To anyone who would listen, Rabin announced that he would take the Fifth Amendment before the committee. Friends said things like, *I'll bake you a cake with a file in it.* His parents were terrified.

Enough with the editorials already, said Lazar. *Think of your future.*

You'll never be able to get a job, wailed Hannah.

You always taught me to look out for the little guy, said Rabin. *To support what's right. You believe in equality.*

Belief is one thing, doing another. Life isn't a bowl of cherries. You have to be careful.

Think of what happened to your poor Uncle Izzy. You don't want to end up like him.

Who's Uncle Izzy? asked Rabin.

· · · ⎯⎯⎯⎯

Only once did Cousin Lionel talk to me about his decade in the Communist Party. This was one time more than he ever discussed the subject with any of his three children or any other member of the family. It was the summer just after my defeat in the campus-wide election for *Daily Bruin* editor, an election in which my editorials and my membership in the NAACP were used widely up and down The Row as proof that I was a Commie. We were sitting in his Morris Minor at the Westmount lookout and watching the lights of Montreal glisten in the summer rain when he began to talk of the past. First the departure scene on the dock. He remembers his thin gloves, his frozen hands, his vow not to shed tears, a vow he managed to keep for almost twenty-four hours; he remembers best of all the wonderful taste of the enormous juicy steak—*the largest I had ever seen*—that Lazar treated him and his mother to at Moishe's right after the ship sailed; he remembers the weight of Lazar's arm thrown around his shoulder, and the words: *Can you eat another one?* He pauses to relish something. *Your father. What a guy. The gangster who wasn't good enough for our Hannah, and he turns out to be the only one with a conscience and a heart. I'll never forget that steak.*

Then Lionel speaks of the lonely years, the now deceased father he would never see, the brother who is so far away, the beliefs that took him into the Party, the desires for justice, freedom, equality; the realities of Party life, the cell meetings, the fractions, the bitter quarrels, the hatreds; the investigations by the Mounties, the cat-and-mouse sessions of questions and answers; the doubts that surface and are pushed away and surface again; the small betrayals and then the big betrayal that ends it all. History, it turns out, is not driven by economics but irony. The man who has been a lifelong atheist falls on the sword of religion. Shortly after the end of the war, at a meeting on upcoming contract negotiations of the sort Lionel has successfully led for six years, a French-speaking worker rises to say that

Izzy the Red 173

since Comrade Borozovitch is not really a worker, he should not be the one to represent them in talks with management. *Not a worker,* Lionel replies. *Not a worker? I've been on the line for years.* His antagonist persists: *It's not your job, it's your nationality, comrade. You are a cosmopolitan and therefore not a true worker!* When the meeting accepts the argument by voice vote, Lionel walks out of the Party, the union, and his job.

Rabin is making sympathetic noises, but Lionel will have none of them. It's water under the bridge. Not important. What really interests him is Hannah. How is she? How is her life? Does she still play the piano? Is she still graceful and lovely? And then he begins to tell a story, the story of a moment, one of those moments that, Rabin will learn years later, can stay with you forever, a simple moment that changes your sense, your very definition of yourself, that teaches you what it is to long for something you will never have, a moment that creates mingled feelings of desire and fulfillment that will never again come together so simply and easily. Teenage Hannah is visiting the Borozovitch family in St. John's, New Brunswick, when Lionel one day opens the door to the bedroom. Does he do it by mistake, does he know she is there, naked to the waist, looking at herself in the mirror? When the image of her younger cousin suddenly appears, Hannah does not scream or cover herself, but instead cups her breasts in her hands and turns slowly toward Lionel and looks him directly in the eye and asks in a voice whose tone he will never forget, *Don't you think I'm beautiful?*

Boris doesn't want to talk about the Party either, though he is still a member in 1972 and, apparently, proud of it. Proud too of his country and its accomplishments. Fidel Castro has visited the Soviet Union a few days before Rabin's arrival there; pineapples are plentiful at stands in the streets, and Boris points to them as a wonderful example of *socialist solidarity.* Tentatively, Rabin raises a delicate issue: anti-Semitism in the Soviet Union. Boris waves away the question. Jews have created the problems for themselves. Everyone is treated equally here. But some Jews, financed by Zionists, are troublemakers, petty nationalists who demand special privileges. Their complaints make troubles for those of us of Jewish background who have nothing to do with religion. They need to stop whining and go about their business. Once the government can get the paperwork done, all such malcontents will be out of the country and in Israel, where they belong with other imperialists.

Political questions seem to annoy Boris. What he wants to talk about is American writers like Steinbeck, Hemingway, and Richard Wright. What he wants to talk about are Western magazines: did Rabin bring any with him, possibly *Playboy*? Or the Beatles: has Rabin seen them in person? (No.) Does he have their records? (Several.) Are they really the biggest thing in Western music? (That depends.) Boris is generous with his time; he takes Rabin to the Tretyakov Gallery, and the Bolshoi, and the Lenin Library; he serves as his translator when Rabin meets fellow historians at the Academy of Science; he treats him to lunch (some sort of goulash with very tough meat) at the Composer's Union dining room; he brings him home to his tiny three-room flat. They gaze out of his ninth-floor apartment at the monsters of the Moscow skyline, and Boris pours a glass of kvass. Despite the bitter taste, Rabin is grateful for the cool drink. Moscow is suffering a July heat wave, and it was a very long walk to and from the butcher shop where there was no meat or chicken and the grocery store where all the produce was gone except for tomatoes, and then a stiff climb up the stairs to the apartment. Boris is full of apologies: *The elevator—it was working this morning; it must have just broken down.*

A dinner of salad and eggs lets him remember the past, speak of the hardships of growing up without a mother, of the army, the Battle of Moscow, the painful months in hospitals, and then, late in the evening, the separation scene in that distant past. What he remembers best is the fifty-dollar bills. All that money stunned his father, who added them to a bunch of other stuff in the money belt strapped around his waist. All through the three-week voyage he kept taking out the fifties and riffling through them once or twice a day as if he couldn't quite believe they were real. Boris never saw the money after they got to Russia. *But they must have been a lifesaver in those early months when we had no income and he couldn't find any of his old friends and it was the middle of winter—Moscow winter, you don't know, you don't want to know. That's the only thing I regret—that my father was in such a hurry to get here that he couldn't wait for summer. Maybe if he had been more patient, more cautious; maybe if the weather were better, he could have convinced mother to come too. That would have been wonderful. But he was always very impatient. When he decided to do something, it had to be done immediately if not sooner.*

. . .⸻

At the height—or should one say the depth?—of the Cold War, long before Rabin or anyone else he knew had ever heard of a private citizen going to the Soviet Union, Aunt Henrietta made a trip to Moscow. Before making travel plans, she had to undergo long interviews with representatives of the American State Department and of the Soviet Embassy, and then she had to wait for more than a year for her visa to be approved. She returned after two months to find reporters waiting to interview her at the airport. Their questions were simple: What is life like there? Aren't the people suffering? Aren't they starving? Don't they all want to come to America? Her answers were direct. Life there is fine. People are busy. They're not as rich as us, but they have free health care and free universities and plenty of food and long vacations. The newspapermen were not happy with these answers, and a sense that Henrietta was a demented old woman or, possibly, a leftist fellow traveler crept into their reports.

Henrietta was neither demented nor a fellow traveler, but she was fearful that her son the composer, well known for his ballet based on musical themes from Iberia and incidents in the Spanish Civil War, might suffer some sort of reprisals if she were in any way critical of the Soviet system. He had, she knew, already suffered enough from his parent's actions. In truth, Henrietta was shocked at the real shortages and shortcomings she saw in the Soviet Union, at her son's dingy apartment, at the lack of heating, the poor food, the rough toilet paper, the constant propaganda in the newspapers and on the radio, and the cringing fear of government officials that Boris exhibited in even the most routine encounters with policemen or bureaucrats.

Henrietta also learned the truth of the old adage, the more things change the more they stay the same. Remarried for some years now to a gentle gentile German refugee, she had no plans to meet with her former husband. But when Boris said Izzy was ill and in bed and wanted very much to see her, she was curious enough to make a trip to his apartment. Face to face in that tiny bedroom, Izzy began to plead, then threatened: She was his wife. She had betrayed him by staying in Canada. He had his rights. He wanted to have sex with her right now—or else. Her negative response made him begin to raise his hand, but the physically stronger Henrietta gently pushed him away. He began to cry softly, then to heave with huge sobs as tears stained his grizzled cheeks. After that they sat on the bed and talked. Or, to be more precise, he complained, she listened. After twenty years he had still not obtained any employment or the social benefits due a Soviet citizen with a regular job—*What kind of a Workers' State is it that can't find a place for a good worker like me?* In all those years since arriving he had lived on the margins. By setting up the old sewing machine he had carried from Canada, he managed to earn a few rubles a month mending the old clothes of various neighbors and people they recommended.

When Izzy went off to the bathroom, Henrietta was left chatting with some of the elderly folk who lived in the communal apartment. They were curious about her, about Canada, about Izzy's background. *We don't know why he came here,* one of them said. *And neither does he. All he has talked about for years now are the wonders of Canada, its landscape, his relatives, the food, the decent way workers are treated.* Now you take St. John's, New Brunswick, *he keeps saying to all of us.* It's not like here. People in New Brunswick are civilized and cultured and have good taste. In St. John's everyone knows how to appreciate the work of a really good tailor.

The author on his first trip to Paris in 1958. He likes to think
that he looks something like his grandfather, Chaim Baer.

— ELEVEN —

Café Odessa

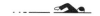

Riots beneath the Chestnut Trees

I went to Paris last spring for the same reasons that people have always gone to Paris. I wanted to see the chestnut trees blooming along the boulevards and the lovers walking hand in hand on the quais of the Seine. I wanted to sit for hours reading free newspapers in sidewalk cafés, and to watch the avant garde painters on the streets of Montmartre. I wanted to browse endlessly through open bookstalls, talk to existentialists in St. Germain and see firsthand the sinning of wicked Pigalle.

I went to Paris in the spring and found instead what I should have expected. Oh the trees were there and so were the lovers. The cafés were fun to sit in all right, but I never got a newspaper for less than 30 francs. The street painters would only be considered avant garde if they had been painting in the 19th century. The books were mostly in French, too difficult for me to translate without a great amount of labor at a dictionary, so I was forced to confine my reading activity to unexpurgated versions of Henry Miller and D. H. Lawrence. When I got to the Café Deux Magots at St. Germain des Pres, Jean Paul Sartre's old hangout, I was told that the honest to goodness existentialists had long since vanished from the area. And the sinning of Pigalle turned out to be the same as sinning anywhere....

But still, it was Paris and it was spring. It was not exactly the Paris of the travel guides, and so some of my illusions were shattered.... There was still French politics to behold, if nothing else, and at least in this sphere I was not disappointed. In fact the French at that time really did things up right. The most I had hoped for was the collapse of a government or two, perhaps a short period of anarchy and maybe some street riots. But what I got was a real spectacular, a complete political upheaval in every sense of the word, with daily public demonstrations, the death of an entire republic, the threat of invasion by paratroopers from Algeria and the beginning of a question mark future.

That, to my mind, will always be Paris in the spring. When I tell my stories I shall leave the chestnut trees to others.

ESSAY BY RABIN ROTENSTEIN,
UCLAN REVIEW MAGAZINE, WINTER 1958–59

*T*here are stories and there are stories, and mine is like any other: if there's one version of it, there are a thousand versions, and who's to know which is the real one. Or if there is a real one. Take the version that my grandson wrote. Not bad for a kid who was not born until thirty years after my death, and hasn't done much real research, and knows me only from hearing all those tales my son, Lazar, began to remember after his mind had drifted into the sweet fogs of age. Or from those crazy stories that Moishe's wife elaborated out of the whoppers that he, my first son, enjoyed telling after he got rich. Like the one that I was a tailor for royalty—as if Romania ever had any real royalty and not just the offspring of some minor German princes who couldn't find a decent job anywhere else on the Continent.

In his own way Rabin didn't do too badly, but how could he really know? You'll notice certain holes in his story. Like a decent explanation for why I left Odessa in the first place, or just what I did during that year in Paris. The former he frankly hasn't much thought about—as if he assumes leaving Odessa was a most natural thing to do. Well, it wasn't. For Russian Jews in that era there could be no better place to live. But a hundred years later, to those who don't know its special history, Odessa may seem like just another drab part of Eastern Europe.

About Paris, Rabin has been far more curious. Lord knows how many times he's written chapters that attempt to give a sense of my life there—a special, charmed life (in his eyes) for a grandfather, a life that somehow prefigures and justifies his own efforts to play at bohemian, artist, and radical in the Latin Quarter. You're lucky you haven't read these chapters. For my money, they're too full of stuff left over from the history classes that he teaches. Rabin writes about Louis-Napoléon, and he writes about Daguerre's early photos of the city, and he even writes about the meshuggane antics of Tristan Tzara, who was—so Rabin says—born in Moinesti, the very town in Romania where I raised the kids. As if all this has something to do with me. These chapters are also too full of inflated stories about Rabin's own amorous episodes with women, French and American. Me?—what he gives his grandfather are a few quickies with hookers, a lingering passion for a Pigalle professional with a twisted mouth, and a mild dose of the clap. My grandson, the scholar! If he only knew.

So let me try to set the record straight. Let me tell you that my hometown, Odessa, was a very special place, a unique place—for many people, it seemed the promised land. All over Eastern Europe you could hear people saying in voices full of wonder: To live like a god in Odessa. Jews are of course always finding promised lands. Remember the original one—some promise! Milk and honey, fine, but no vegetation. Trees, grass, flowers—you think He would be able to provide a few of those too, just to soften the view of sand and rocky hills. Babylonia was another promised land, at least for all except the zealots who wanted to hold on to the memory of Jerusalem. Spain, Lithuania, Poland—all for a time were marvelous promised lands that only proved in the end that He doesn't keep all his promises any more than anyone else.

In the nineteenth century Odessa was a boomtown, Russia's first warm-water port, her answer to Marseilles, a place for shipping the grain of the steppes to the entire world. Jews came here from everywhere—from all over the Pale of Settlement, from Brody, Lvov, Tarnapol; from a thousand tiny villages made up of mud, flies, and oppression. All sorts of people—not just Jews—came to this city of opportunity from the far reaches of the Russian Empire and beyond—from Italy, Turkey, Greece, North Africa. In Odessa the lives of Jews were not so circumscribed as they were everywhere else in Russia. In Odessa there was no ghetto and few restrictive laws. In Odessa we had not just Jewish merchants and businessmen and laborers, but Jewish politicians, city councilmen, policemen. In Odessa we had Jewish radicals and gangsters. These last two groups—they're the real reason I had to leave. It was not, as Rabin suggests, that I wanted to *avoid military service or get away from my family. True, he makes a good guess in saying that the family and I never got on very well. Why? Don't ask me. Don't even ask me who they were, where they were from, what they did. They were a family like any other, nice enough people in their own way—but it wasn't my way. The only one that I really found interesting was an uncle, the one who boarded a ship bound for Southeast Asia and never returned. Now he, I used to think (and I still think), he must have some stories to tell.*

You know what I remember best about Odessa—what really sticks in my mind? Not the broad boulevards with their cafés, not the elegant stores with goods imported from France and England; not the grand staircase down to the harbor or the opera house or the glorious views of the Black Sea from the esplanade, not even the incessant arguments at the temple or the endless political wrangling. What I remember best about Odessa is the dust. Gottenu! *The dust was worse than the pogroms. At least they were occasional, but the dust was always there, day after day, year after year, spring, summer, and fall. In winter it was different. Then it rained and rained, and there was no dust—there was mud. Mud that covered your shoes; mud that covered the wheels of carts, mud that came up to your thighs, mud that would make horses slip and carts overturn; mud that could drown children and short adults.*

When I was born Odessa was already a city of a quarter million, already a major center for the garment industry. So I was only one of many young boys apprenticed by his parents, right after bar mitzvah, to become a tailor. You have to understand that the world of tailors was a huge one—five thousand journeymen with apprentices, assistants, helpers, wives and kids. Now, to be a tailor in Odessa was to be something. A tailor was not just a worker but a man with an important skill, a mind, and aspirations for a better life—for a bigger shop or a small factory, for kids who might become doctors or concert violinists. To be a young tailor in Odessa in the 1880s was to live a cultured life, a life you might recognize even today. We went to lectures on art, socialism, evolution, political reform, and vegetarianism; we attended the theater, concerts, and the Opera, and always came away humming romantic arias in Italian. We read newspa-

pers in Yiddish or, some of us, in Russian; we belonged to the pub-
lic library, where we entered the worlds of Turgenev, Chekhov, and
Gorky, of Balzac, Stendahl, and Dickens. We young tailors in Odessa
went down to the sea to swim—what? You really thought my famous
swim across the Prut River was the first time? We sat in outdoor
cafés on De Ribas Boulevard, roamed the streets of the Moldavanka
on summer nights, stopping in bars to drink and play cards and then
ended up, in the early hours of the morning, at Rosenthal's, where
you could buy a few moments or a few hours of passion with a blonde
whose cheekbones suggested that she might indeed be, as Rosenthal
claimed, pure-blooded Russian.

For a young Jewish single man in Odessa, the Moldavanka was his
home, and Greek Street was the center of the district. That's where
my pleasures were taken, that's where my troubles (if troubles they
were) began. Greek Street was lined with bars and gambling houses—
they were all the same, equally noisy, equally full of drunken work-
men, cheap whores, two-bit gangsters, pale yeshiva students, Gypsy
violinists, radicals, informers, revolutionaries. For us, such a mixture
was nothing new. In Odessa the world was changing. We were break-
ing away from our histories; we were trying on new sorts of lives. Our
passions for gambling or changing the world or sleeping with Rus-
sian women were not seen as contradictory—all were part of a lib-
eration from the cramped world of our fathers, the world of cringing
and second-class citizenship that we Jews of Odessa had left (or so
we were certain) far behind.

My regular hangout in the Moldavanka was Lyubka's. A bunch of
us in our twenties would gather there almost every evening to drink,
gamble, and talk. Everyone seemed capable of talking a mile a min-
ute and making sense. Of course, almost everyone there was Jewish.
What did you expect? Freer we might be in Odessa than anywhere
else in Russia, but that didn't mean that we mingled with goyim, ex-
cept maybe on the job. Oh, there were always stories about one of ours,
some daughter or son of a rich merchant, who became the hit of one
of their balls, or who married one of them. And for a while a bunch
of liberal Jewish optimists—you know the kind—formed a club where
we were supposed to meet with them on a regular basis to discuss so-

cial and cultural subjects of mutual interest. It only lasted for a year. The Us and Them never really changed.

If life was so good in Odessa, you're thinking, why did I leave? It's not what you think. Say you left Russia, and someone is sure to say pogroms. Jews have pogroms on the brain. Especially Jews of a later generation, Jews like my grandson Rabin. They seem to think that pogroms were all that we thought about, that we sat around daily wondering if a pogrom was about to happen. Don't get me wrong: from pogroms I know; from atrocities too. Destruction, homelessness, injury, death—in 1871, 1881, 1905—these were pogroms enough to satisfy the gloomiest of doomsayers. But life is life. In parts of the world people live on faults in the earth, and they don't spend all their time worrying about the next big tremor. Earthquakes don't define their existence; pogroms didn't define ours. I left Odessa in 1886—five years after one bad pogrom, nineteen years before a worse one. To tell you the truth, the latter had about as much to do with my leaving as did the former.

The story of why I left begins in Lyubka's. More than a bar, this was a social center, a school, an ongoing seminar in ideas and life. All kinds of people gathered here, and all sorts of roles were mixed together. A man might be a cobbler or a second-story man by day, but in Lyubka's at night he was an anarchist or a philosopher or a revolutionary. Since the government treated radicals and criminals much the same, it's little wonder that the worlds overlapped. No, that's not quite true. The Russian government, like any government, tolerated— even needed—certain kinds of criminals: those who took care of social tasks like gambling, prostitution, fixing contracts, getting rid of enemies. But radicals? Despotic or democratic, no government will tolerate them for very long.

Me?—let's just say I was a little of both. Tailor by day, gambler, drinker, and parlor radical by night. My buddies—who knew exactly what they did away from Lyubka's? And who would be so impolite as to ask? To share a vodka or two, a hand or an evening of cards, or a woman can be less intimate than to share the secrets of someone's authentic beliefs. All I can tell you is that one night I was playing cards with, among other people, Zeldovich and Hertzstein, and the next night they weren't around and someone mentioned that the police had picked them up. *Six of us at a table looked at each other with eyes full of questions. Oistrakh was missing the next night, and the day after that my landlady said that some unknown, suspicious person had come to the door to ask questions about me.*

True, I was guilty of nothing. True, I could stay and fight whatever imaginary case that officials might make against me (and we had good lawyers in Odessa), but as always in Russia, who knew exactly what would happen when a Jew—or when anyone—stepped into court? Besides, I had other reasons for taking this opportunity to get away, if only for a while. I was young, full of healthy spirits, ready to see a bit of the world. Paris—how long had I dreamed of going there? For lots of us, France itself was a kind of dream—the land of the revolution that set us free, the first country to allow us to become citizens, doctors, even military officers. Dreyfuss, you ask? This was the mid-eighties, remember? His trials were still in the future.

So what my grandson doesn't know and can't even imagine is that when I left Odessa I was on my way to Paris. How did I know it would take so many years to get there? Life! It has a way of disrupting your plans. Not that mine were so well laid. But to tell the truth, I don't know whether to be tickled or angered to think that my grandson actually believes I was escaping Odessa to live in Romania. You'd have to be crazy to do that! Crazy even if you were about to be drafted into the czar's service. To choose between twenty years in the Russian army and a lifetime in Romania would be a close call. Not only would you live much longer in Romania, it would seem much, much longer. Yet you are right to wonder how, after a long hike and after my famous swim across the Prut River, I got stuck in Romania. A very good question—one that I still can wonder about myself. One that's not so easy to answer.

Twenty years in Romania—you know how twenty years go? As quickly as a dream. You are a single man. You get a woman pregnant. You think yourself a man of honor. You lie to yourself. In the face of all the evidence of twenty-seven years of living (which is not, after all, very long), or five thousand years of history (which is), in the face of all the evidence that says we are all the same, all caught by life—you say: me, I'm different. I'm free. I'll marry her and in a couple of years I'll continue—we'll continue the journey to Paris together. Tell me another good one. She gets pregnant again and the kids are cute (at first) and helpless (for a long time) and—do I have to tell you? Don't we all know the story too well? The difference now is that it's happening to you.

This I want you to believe: for twenty years in Romania, Paris was never entirely out of my mind. I know, I know: a jaunt to Paris is not part of your image of a Jewish grandfather. Better I should be in the temple, studying holy texts; better I should be off to America to give my kids a proper start on the ladder of success. Later I would do all that. Like everyone else, I would make that trip to America. But first it was Paris. Do I know the story of how I was turned back at Ellis Island? Of course I know it! I made it up! But it was only a story for my neighbors, for the children, for Sarah. Everyone else believed it, but not her. Not for a minute. Women have a way of knowing things— don't ask me how. They just do. But she never breathed a word of it to the kids, not to her dying day. And so my grandchildren—even the historian Rabin—would believe that I became this unusual Jewish grandfather by accident. But it was no accident. I didn't just happen to end up in Paris. I went to Paris because I wanted to go there.

But Sarah, she knew. Knew though I never so much as wavered one moment from the story, never altered a single detail. Maybe that's how she knew. Any other story I would change, elaborate, improve each time. Like the one about swimming the Prut River. Sometimes it was an easy swim; sometimes difficult; sometimes I waded because the water was so shallow. Sometimes it took me half an hour, sometimes half a day. Sometimes I was almost swept away by the roaring spring current, sometimes battered by ice floes. Sometimes a peasant saved me from drowning, sometimes I saved a rabbi who couldn't swim. So many versions that I forgot the original details myself.

The story of the trip to the New World never varied. Each time I went to Vienna, Paris, and Rotterdam; each time boarded the SS Karlsruhe (I checked it in the papers, the sailing schedule, the weather); each time the same seasickness and the same immigration officer at Ellis Island turns me back: on his list as an anarchist terrorist is another Chaim Baer Rotenstein from Romania. The first ship back is always the Isle de France, *bound for Le Havre, and there, on a drizzly September day, I am alone in that gray French port with just enough money for a third-class ticket to Paris, a simple plate of onion soup and bread at the station buffet, and one night in the cheapest of hotels, where I share a bed with a Ukrainian cobbler who has eaten way too much garlic for dinner, even by Rumanian standards. The next day—why, thank God for the Israelite Alliance. They advance me money, find me a job in a sweat shop, pay in advance for a room, which I share with a kosher butcher from Iasi. But of course there is a catch. A small one. It takes a whole year of work to pay back my debt to the Alliance.*

Of this whole story, Sarah never believed a word, though she could hardly have guessed the real truth—that I had planned to go to Paris all along. How to explain this simply or directly. There was the original impulse, but that was years ago and now something else was also at work. Let's say a man never loses his dreams. Let's say he gets to a certain age. He has a nice life—a wife who can cook and keep him warm at night; a bunch of bright, good-looking boys and girls; a steady income; a house; some books; a good game of cards every Saturday night. It's what he has worked for—maybe too well. And so there comes a day when he wants something else, when his earlier dreams return with a new urgency. The years ahead of him, full as they are, look empty too. And that emptiness can begin to grow, expand until it is larger than any fullness he feels.

Such careful planning it took. For a year I read aloud at the dinner table articles about opportunities in America, where there were no laws against us and Jews were treated just like anyone else. What I hid were the books on France. Not that Sarah would have known what they were about, for she couldn't read Russian or Romanian. So I planned. I plotted. I saved so that the family would not be without. And then on a bright August morning, with real tears in my eyes (of sorrow to leave Sarah and the young ones, and joy that this dream was beginning at last, and fear of what if, what if); on that glorious morning full of the late summer smell of vineyards and cornfields, I left Tetscani in an oxcart driven by a peasant on his way to Bacau. Everything was going according to plan, and it would stay that way through Bucharest and Vienna and along nine hundred miles of railroad track. The months ahead would make up just the year I had planned too, except for one surprise:

Her name was Ruth.

Talk about the power of names. There she was, amidst the alien corn. To be truthful: cornmeal. To be Romanian: mamaliga. The one and only thing that unites that nation. Racial, religious, regional, and class lines all disappear in steaming pots of cornmeal mush. History, the constitution, the great national tradition of taking anything that isn't nailed down, none of this links Romanians together as much as a taste for mamaliga—hot or cold, with gravy or cheese, heaped on platters or rolled into a nice ball and carried in the pocket to be nibbled during the day. In the sixteenth century, Vlad the Third, nicknamed Prince Dracula, ate mamaliga to quell the appetite he worked up during long sessions devoted to impaling vanquished enemies. In the nineteenth, the patriarch of Eastern Orthodoxy in Bucharest and the chief rabbi of Iasi debated theological issues while sharing a simple meal of mamaliga. On each New Year's Day in the twentieth, whichever King Carol was in power would force himself to eat a bowl of it. During the Great War, in the secrecy of his Zurich hotel room, Tristan Tzara, while waiting for the mamaliga to boil, would amuse himself by cutting words out of newspapers, stuffing them into a bag, and writing them down on paper in the order that he pulled them forth. When the mamaliga was done, so was his poem.

Ruth? How to tell you about Ruth? Where to begin? With the delicatessen where we met on Rue des Juifs in the Marais? It was the third week of my stay. Already I had a job. A room. Already I had walked the Champs-Elysées, visited the Louvre, sat in cafés enjoying the bitter coffee and sweet aperitifs, spent an afternoon in the Bois de Boulogne, lingered outside the Moulin Rouge and the Chat Noir, fearful of the expense of entering. The Folies Bergere were my big splurge. Can you imagine my excitement at what was right before me on the stage? Never had I seen such a display of female flesh. With Sarah, with other women, it was always in the dark. To tell the truth, in Odessa even the hookers liked to cover up their bodies. So the Folies was a revelation of another realm of possibilities, another sort of life.

And yet. You know how it is when you are far away from home. No matter how good a time you are having, at moments the sweet realities of what you have left behind stab at you—wife, kids, friends, the sound of a rooster, the vistas of hills that define your life, even the boundaries that you had to flee: all seem full of a special feeling that spreads out onto people, objects, landscapes. The joy of the Folies, the visions of those naked bodies, so near, so far, left me feeling alone, lost, sorry for myself because I was here only playing at life, escaping my own reality. You know the feeling? The Folies left me empty, weary of croissants and the crunch of baguettes, longing for bread of more substance, bread less like a dream and more like reality, bread dark and heavy like a more familiar life.

Ruth. What can I tell you about her? That she was an exile from Poland. A radical tired of the company of other radicals. Beautiful? All these things were important, but when you are forty-six and away from home in Paris, none of the details really make a difference. Not later; not when you've come to understand how much you created her. Such a statement surprises you? What, you think, does an old-country grandfather know of midlife problems? Let alone from passion, instant desire, hunger for a young lady standing behind the counter of a delicatessen, her piled-up hair spilling out of a babushka (suddenly such a sexy garment). Here's another surprise: we right away recognized each other. At a glance, without a word, we knew what would be—the intensity, the desperation, the longing. Not that this knowing was in words; not that it helped; not that it would make either of us say no to that moment or to walk away from it.

No doubt it was our ages. We were not exactly kids. At forty-six you know what you know, and you know that what you don't know you'll never know. Ruth was not yet forty, but in those days a woman at forty, or a man at forty-six—remember, there were no refrigerators, no vitamins, no notion that you are what you eat. And even if we had such a notion, there was no money to indulge dietary whims, no time for exercise. We used salt on everything and ate anything that tasted good—meat, butter, and eggs as much and as often as possible; cookies, strudel, and honey cake; lots of glasses of tea with lots of sugar; and for a special snack on Shabbas, black bread and plenty of herring with a few shots of schnapps. By her thirties a woman's body, even if, like Ruth, she did not have children, sagged and wrinkled. A man, if he was prosperous or lucky, didn't sag so much as bulge. When you have that instant knowing that we did, it is no doubt a mitzvah. But if you are smart—and God somehow blessed us with smarts beyond our experience—you will still go through all the proper moments, for the going is what makes the moments what they are. So everything happened as you might imagine, as I had imagined ever since making the decision for Paris. There in a room full of the steam, the heat, the clatter of dishes, the clash of voices in French, Polish, Russian, Yiddish, Latvian, Romanian, discussing, arguing, promoting, denouncing, complaining; in the glaring yellow light, amidst the shoving waiters, the intense crush of unwashed bodies, our eyes meet. Do you know the erotics of the glance? The quick look back again. The steady gaze. The stirring sound of a Slavic voice.

I don't remember our first words and I don't remember any of the later ones. Strange. God knows we talked, we never stopped talking. With Ruth I talked more words than I knew were in me, but none remain. Does it matter? Do any of the details matter? How necessary is it to remember the looks, the touches, the words? What would you know, what would I know, if I listed the restaurants (not very fancy ones) where we ate, the streets where we walked; if I pointed with geographical precision to each particular bench where we sat in the Jardin des Plantes, or on the quays of the Seine; if I wrote down the name of every boulangerie where we bought pain au chocolate, every steaming stand in the Latin Quarter where we purchased a sugarcoated crepe. Love is always love—its moments the moments of love. And if you don't know its moments, how could I explain them to you? Middle-aged love is the same as any other only the illusions and hopes are gone, leaving moments that happen all too quickly.

Listen, I wouldn't want you to think I was wholly without a conscience. Happy as Ruth made me, sometimes on a Sunday when we could not be together, and I wandered with no thought for tomorrow's hours at the sewing machine, sometimes I would begin to worry. About what I was doing here. About my foolishness. About betraying my family or ideas I learned so long ago in Odessa. Things I had *believed as a young man, ideas I had not much remembered in recent years but which knowing Ruth had brought back to me—that the wealth was given by God to everyone equally, but that the few had stolen it, piled it away in their mansions, factories, and banks. Yet surely the ones who insisted on such ideas in meeting halls, and synagogues, and coffeehouses, surely they too would change their tune if they had to spend two decades in Romania. Twenty years of Gypsies and* mamaliga *must surely entitle a man to a piece of delicate pastry or the taste of a young lady or to some heart-rending months of love.*

You think I was engaged in another, more personal form of betrayal? Remember the words of the Talmud: A man will have to answer in the next world for all the pleasures he refused in this one without sufficient cause. *What did Ruth ever take away from Sarah and the kids? After the first bunch of flowers, she refused to accept any sort of gift. In truth, I spent more on my sweet tooth than on her. You shouldn't think the family ever lost an iota of my affection. Never for an instant did I stop missing them, the three boys and four girls, missing them so much that the missing surprised me.* Mein kinder *I would moan to myself when the beauty of a woman in a passing carriage stabbed into me.* Sometimes I cannot remember your faces, and you will have grown, changed so much, become different people by the time I return. *But then, just in case, I would silently add for the benefit of He Who Watches over Us:* Don't get me wrong. Don't play one of your famous tricks and answer what might sound like a prayer. It's not that at all. Indulge me for a while longer, and I may come to believe in You. When I go home it will be to care for them for the rest of my life. I promise. But don't make it happen too quickly. Let me stay here until I have my fill.

Sometimes in life you're lucky: He did!

After the year in Paris, Montreal was an anticlimax. It had to be. Yes, I could have come back to Paris with the family, found a decent job, seen a nice future for the kids. Such notions crossed my mind. But after that year—Paris without Ruth? Impossible. Paris was Ruth. Her ghost would have haunted me. Or I would have haunted our favorite spots. Like the Café Odessa. Far away from the Jews of the Marais and Montmartre. Close enough to the artists of Montparnasse to feel as if we might be part of them. Full of Russian immigrants. Why did we like it? The Odessa was no different from any other café except that the people spoke a language that was familiar. Which meant that the Odessa seemed to belong to us, and that we really belonged here. Not as transients or visitors, but as people who belonged permanently. As if Paris were really our home. As if we really had a home.

Some Canadians like to call Montreal Little Paris, but to my eyes it was just a cold northern city. As for the tumor on my head that Rabin mentions, it was a matter of medical necessity. The doctors were very clear: the growth was close to the brain; the operation might not succeed. But why bother the family? Why worry them? If they lost me, they would know soon enough, and if I stayed around for a while they shouldn't have had to worry for nothing. I made up the story about the operation being cosmetic for Sarah and the kids. Later, there was nobody around to correct it, but what's the difference? Let them say I died for vanity. It's hardly the worst of sins.

As for my grandson Rabin—for all the mistakes in his writing about me, I sense the gropings of a youngster who wants some message from me. Wants me to tell him what it all meant to me. And by extension: what it should mean to him. Since his father never told him, perhaps he can learn from this mythical grandfather, the hero who swam the Prut River, the romantic who lived in Paris. Well, I hate to disappoint the kid, but like his father, Lazar, I was a never much of a talker either. Except with Ruth, even if I can't remember anything we said. Yet I do remember her last word, spoken just before she turned away and walked briskly down the platform at the Gare du Nord, walked away and—as she had promised, for she hated the idea of tears—never turned around, just walked straight away and disappeared into a third-class coach. She was going home to Warsaw, to her husband; going home to help make the revolution. Which one? What does it matter?—to lovers all revolutions are the same.

The last word was forever.

I guess there is one thing I can tell Rabin, one thing that might serve him well in the years ahead: Don't believe all the stories you hear. But don't disbelieve them either.

Lazar and Rabin, the author, circa 1977.

Sunday in Montreal

S undays could be very special. Sunlight fell across the table where you feasted on orange juice, oatmeal, bacon and eggs, and two slices of toasted rye and maybe a third covered with strawberry jam that mother had boiled in huge pots last summer on the wood-burning stove in the wooden house on Trout Lake the day after everyone had been stung by bees while berrying in the woods, and your stings had been so bad that father had driven into St. Agathe to the doctor with the funny French name that nobody could pronounce, and in spite of what he promised the needle did hurt going into your upper left arm, but the cookies at the bakery with the funny French name that nobody could pronounce helped to sweeten away the pain, and coming along the narrow highway home past the Ferris wheel of the carnival everyone had fun yelling *Get a horse* at the man in the horse-drawn cart going slowly up the long hill into the forest above the lake onto the highway that wound above the shining water through the trees and back to the little house full of the warm smell of all the strawberries in the world. After breakfast father warmed up the car. It was a 1939 Packard, an elegant black with the softest seats of gray, pinstriped velvet. Highways were not crowded in those days, and going toward the foothills of the Laurentian Mountains you could see towns like St. Therese long before you reached them, for suddenly a spire with a cross or the vast dome of a cathedral appeared over the swelling green fields. The car took you to amusement parks and lakes for swimming, to birch forests and Indian towns along the St. Lawrence where tepees were more expressive than the silent people whose stares were so dark and empty, to the secret parking lot behind Blue

Bonnet's where through the broken boards you could almost touch the horses roaring down the backstretch and across the turf and in-field was a grandstand packed with the shirtsleeves of fathers who had never owned a racehorse. The airport was a favorite. From behind a chain-link fence you watched the planes take off and miraculously lift from the earth, sailing into the blue, soaring gloriously, freely, noiselessly toward piles of magic clouds, even on that chilly Sunday when the music on the radio was interrupted by an excited voice and an even more excited father slammed his fist onto the dashboard and shouted, *Now those goddamn Americans can't stay out. They've got to get in it now.*

Only once did you visit the graveyard. It was very green, very overgrown, very still. Sunlight splotched unevenly on the grass and the granite headstones. Father fussed, complained, worried out loud. Everything was uncared-for, untidy, wrong. There were no flowers and mother refused to accompany him here and even his brothers would not come anymore. The undertaker was a crook; he charged a fortune for upkeep and look how awful things were, so awful he would certainly not pay the next yearly bill. He held your hand, but father seemed somewhere far away. You stopped at a large plot, large enough for half a dozen people, but here there was only one stone, with the inscription *Seymour Rotenstein—1934.* Your elder brother, you knew that already, knew he had lived only a few months and that you were his replacement on earth. God had taken him away so soon because, as your mother always said, he was too good for this world. Father led you on a very long walk to a section so crowded and jumbled with tilting stones, long grass and scraggly bushes that it was difficult for him to find the right place, which proved to be in front of an old, weathered stone whose inscription was in Hebrew, like the prayer books in temple. For a long, long time looking at the stone, your father did not speak, did not move. His expression was so sad, unfamiliar, so foreign, so strange that you were beginning to become frightened when at last he said two words: *Chaim Baer.* Was that a tear in your father's eye? *My father. His name was Chaim Baer.* You did not say a word as the two of you left the cemetery and drove home along Decarie. He stopped the car at Miss Montreal and bought you a cone with two scoops of your favorite ice cream: maple. Later, much later you would realize that was the first time you had ever heard your father speak of his own father. The first time you realized that your father must have had a father too.